SILVER
IS THE NEW
OIL

SILVER
IS THE NEW
OIL

Strategies for Profiting From the Next Industrial Revolution

COLLIN PLUME

Founder and CEO of Noble Gold Investments

Published by Best Seller Publishing®, St. Augustine, FL
Best Seller Publishing® is a registered trademark.
Printed in the United States of America.

ISBN: 978-1-966395-04-1

This publication is designed to provide accurate and authoritative information with regard to the subject matter covered. It is sold with the understanding that the publisher is not engaged in rendering legal, accounting, or other professional advice. If legal advice or other expert assistance is required, the services of a competent professional should be sought. The opinions expressed by the author in this book are not endorsed by Best Seller Publishing® and are the sole responsibility of the author rendering the opinion.

For more information, please write:
Best Seller Publishing®
1775 US-1 #1070
St. Augustine, FL 32084
or call 1 (626) 765-9750
Visit us online at: www.BestSellerPublishing.org

Dedicated to Sharon, Max, Mina, and Mason:
This journey is for you and because of you.

About the Author

Collin Plume is a renowned expert in the precious metals industry, specializing in helping investors achieve outsized returns with minimized risk. With over two decades of experience, he has guided clients in building and preserving wealth through alternative assets.

As a serial entrepreneur, Collin has founded successful ventures, including Noble Gold Investments—one of the leading precious metals and IRA brokerages—and My Digital Money, a cutting-edge cryptocurrency IRA trading platform.

Beyond his professional success, Collin is also a dedicated husband and father of three, and his family-first values influence his business approach. He prioritizes integrity and a genuine commitment to each client's financial well-being, making him a trusted guide in navigating complex financial markets.

With his deep expertise and strategic approach, Collin assists clients in diversifying into alternative assets like precious metals, real estate, and digital currencies. He believes that leveraging these less-correlated assets alongside traditional investment vehicles provides the perfect balance of protection and wealth generation.

Disclaimer

This book is intended for entertainment purposes only and does not constitute financial advice.

All investments carry risks, including market volatility, economic changes, and potential value fluctuations. Before making investment decisions, thoroughly research your options and conduct due diligence.

To manage risk, avoid putting all your financial resources into a single investment. Diversifying across multiple assets can help mitigate risks and enhance portfolio stability.

Always understand the details of your investments and consult with a qualified financial professional.

Remember, past performance is not necessarily indicative of future results.

Consider your risk tolerance and personal financial situation before investing.

Table of Contents

Foreword

As a longtime observer of the precious metals market—especially silver—I've encountered countless perspectives and predictions about the future of this versatile metal. Few have captured the essence of silver's potential as vividly and persuasively as Collin has in his book, *Silver Is the New Oil*.

In these pages, Collin presents silver's true nature: not only as an investment opportunity but as a cornerstone of our technological future and an irreplaceable resource in the global pivot to sustainable energy. His assertion that silver will rival oil in economic influence is bold yet backed by extensive research and a deep understanding of market dynamics.

What sets this book apart is Collin's ability to interweave multiple, timely threads—technological breakthroughs, geopolitical shifts, environmental demands, and economic trends—to paint a vivid picture of silver's rising importance. He doesn't simply tell us that silver is valuable; he demonstrates how, why, and what it means for our future.

Silver Is the New Oil goes beyond superficial commodity analysis and offers readers a practical roadmap to financial success, sharing insights into proven wealth-building strategies. His 'Satellite City Approach' to real estate investing and his perspectives on business acquisition are noteworthy and provide readers with actionable ways to diversify and grow their wealth.

I find his call to challenge conventional wisdom particularly commendable. In an age where conformity often leads to average outcomes, Collin urges readers to think differently and identify hidden opportunities. This mindset, combined with his practical strategies, equips readers with the tools needed to secure their financial future.

As someone who has long advocated for silver's strategic importance, I view Collin's work as a valuable addition to the ongoing conversation. *Silver Is the New Oil* goes beyond understanding silver's potential—it's about positioning yourself to capitalize on the changes reshaping our economic future.

David Morgan
Founder of The Morgan Report

Introduction

This book is more than a silver investment guide; woven into these pages is a framework for success and wealth generation.

While I believe in the unique financial opportunity the silver market currently presents, I want to show you that you hold the power to create the future you desire.

Silver is one of the many ways to turn your financial dream into reality.

Since 2022, I have noticed a disheartening trend among Americans: a dimming of our entrepreneurial spark. This decline is alarming!

Everyone is looking for an easy way to gain wealth.

Even worse, there's a pervasive thought that the best times are behind us. Americans feel more pressure than ever and believe they have less money, less hope, and fewer opportunities.

This mindset fosters dependency, leading people to seek external solutions rather than taking personal initiative to generate wealth and opportunity.

This attitude has fueled what I call "The Handout Economy."

Americans have become so comfortable receiving handouts and expecting results without working for them that they now view the world as an enemy.

During the pandemic, PPP loans, stimulus checks, and easy money created a false sense of wealth and security.

That window has closed and will not reopen unless a significant economic event or disaster occurs.

It's time to accept that the era of easy money is over and move forward. We can't live hoping someone else will save us.

I want to show you that the world isn't as dim as it appears. Opportunities still exist, waiting to be discovered by those with initiative.

Rather than waiting for help, you must learn to rely on yourself to build the security and financial rewards you want.

In a time of waning generosity, the only handout you should be looking for is the one extended to help you rise and transform adversity into opportunity.

America stands at a critical point. If we continue down this path, we risk losing the entrepreneurial spirit that built our nation. Now, more than ever, we need to reignite our passion for innovation, risk-taking, and small business development.

Our ancestors built the American economy on the belief that ordinary citizens could turn ideas into thriving enterprises. They didn't want a nation of takers. They wanted doers, builders, and givers.

We need to rekindle the flames of ambition and ingenuity.

The American dream is still attainable for those willing to work hard and take calculated risks. I know there's more than enough opportunity for everyone.

The pandemic should have shown us that we don't live in a zero-sum game. The government floods our economy with dollars; all you need is a proven system to extract those dollars from the market and build the life you want.

That's why I wrote this book.

This book has taken many forms over the past few years. Initially, my only goal was to share the massive opportunity I see developing in the precious metals market. However, after completing the first draft, I realized I was doing you a disservice by only discussing the opportunity without showing how to capitalize on it.

I realized I could discuss the opportunity all I wanted, but it meant nothing without giving you the mental framework and systems needed to take advantage of it.

Just telling you silver will double in price is as helpful as handing a novice cook a set of $5,000 chef's knives and expecting them to create a Michelin-star meal.

Sure, you have great tools, but without knowledge and experience, you won't know how to use them effectively.

Realizing my initial mistake, I tore the book apart and started over to provide you with the tools and knowledge needed for success. This is the book I wish I had at the start of my entrepreneurial journey. It's more than a silver investment guide; it's a manual for spotting trends, mitigating risks, and seizing opportunities.

What's contained in these pages?

First, I'll share my insights into one of the most overlooked but highly traded financial markets: **SILVER**.

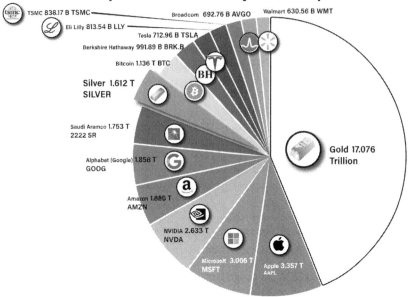

Top 15 Assets Ranked by Market Capitalization

TSMC 838.17 B TSMC

Eli Lilly 813.54 B LLY

Berkshire Hathaway 991.89 B BRK.B

Bitcoin 1.136 T BTC

Silver 1.612 T
SILVER

Saudi Aramco 1.753 T
2222 SR

Alphabet (Google) 1.858 T
GOOG

Amazon 1.886 T
AMZN

NVIDIA 2.633 T
NVDA

Microsoft 3.066 T
MSFT

Apple 3.357 T
AAPL

Broadcom 692.76 B AVGO

Tesla 712.96 B TSLA

Walmart 630.56 B WMT

Gold 17.076
Trillion

As the image above shows, silver's market capitalization rivals that of stocks like Apple, Microsoft, and Amazon. Yet this massive market remains relatively small when you compare average volume and active participants. Blue-chip stocks trade tens of millions of shares daily, while silver sees a small fraction of that activity.

Silver offers significant potential returns for the average investor and stands out as one of the best opportunities in today's investment landscape.

However, if you don't act on this specific opportunity, this book will still provide insights and frameworks for identifying opportunities and distilling them into actionable steps.

In the second part of this book, I'll share my investment philosophy and discuss several unconventional ways I've built wealth for myself and my family. This section provides a roadmap for you to do the same.

Readers will gain the most from this book by integrating both pieces, answering the question I'm asked more than any other: "HOW?"

It usually comes as the question, "How did you build wealth?" or "How did you get rich?"

I will tell you how, but I'll start by saying **my way will never be your way**.

Everyone attempting something audacious or life-changing shares a similar thought: 'If I just knew how my problems would be solved.' I've been there—I used to think that, too. But the more 'hows' I discovered, the more I realized that every path is unique.

So, every time someone asks, "How?" I want to reply, "*How I did it doesn't matter. **HOW ARE YOU GOING TO DO IT?**"*

The truth is, *my "how" will never be your "how."*

My path will never be your path because, in business and in life, no two paths are the same.

So, if you find yourself on a clear, well-defined trail, you're likely following someone else's path—and it probably won't lead you to your desired destination.

The Value of an Entrepreneurial Spirit

We aren't so different. I wasn't born into wealth, nor did I grow up surrounded by extreme privilege. My only advantage was being born into a family with an entrepreneurial spirit, which profoundly shaped my outlook on life.

The story of how this spirit took root in my family is a testament to American ingenuity.

My great-grandparents passed away when my grandfather was young, leaving him, at just fourteen, with no money and three siblings to care for. He didn't have the luxury of waiting for help; he did what he had to survive and started working in a garment factory in downtown Los Angeles.

After years of learning the business, my grandfather took a risk with the knowledge he'd gained and started his own garment company.

Years later, my father, having married into this family of apparel entrepreneurs, learned the trade from his father-in-law (my grandfather on my mom's side) and eventually started his own garment business.

Watching them work tirelessly to build something of their own instilled in me a core belief: opportunity always exists if you're committed to finding a problem and working relentlessly to solve it.

Observing their entrepreneurial journeys taught me that wealth is simply a byproduct of creating solutions to real-world challenges.

*"Strive not to be a success, but
rather to be of value."*
~**ALBERT EINSTEIN**

Their commitment, effort, and perseverance provided an education beyond what any classroom could offer.

I learned there are only a few proven paths to becoming wealthy:

Inherit it.
Marry into it.
Become a high-ranking executive.
Manage other people's money.
Start a business.

If you look at this list and see few viable options, you're not alone. Most of these paths rely on factors beyond our control—odds I've never been comfortable with.

Growing up surrounded by people who worked relentlessly to build something of their own and create a better life, I knew I'd one day start my own business and follow their lead.

While I eventually built a secure future, the journey was far from easy. I faced countless risks and more sleepless nights than raising a newborn.

'Easy' only exists in hindsight. When you're fighting to make a difference, everything feels hard. It's like swimming against the tide with a backpack full of bricks. But I learned early on that anything worthwhile comes with a challenge.

That's why the view from the top of a mountain is far more fulfilling when you've climbed it yourself rather than taking a shortcut to the summit.

Battling to achieve something meaningful is both exhilarating and deeply rewarding, and I want you to experience that same satisfaction.

A Business Machete

I wrote this book to guide you along your path to success. The road you seek isn't clear because you haven't blazed it yet. Creating a new path requires effort, persistence, and a lot of trial and error.

This book is your business machete—a tool for eliminating the unnecessary and creating your path to success. It's my way of giving back, extending a hand to those who, like me, start with empty pockets but a heart full of ambition. It's a roadmap for those who dare to dream big, who refuse to accept the hand life has dealt them, and who are willing to work to reshape their financial future.

In these pages, you'll get a behind-the-scenes look at the grit, resilience, and strategic thinking needed to build lasting wealth. I'll be honest—the path to financial success isn't easy. It demands sacrifice, calculated risks, and the ability to learn from failure. But I promise you the journey is worth every step.

Whether you're just starting out, looking to diversify, or ready to reinvent your financial future, this book is here to inform, inspire, and empower you.

Are you ready to transform your life, uncover hidden opportunities, and join those who turned "someday" into today?

Your journey to financial freedom starts now.

SECTION ONE

Silver's Time
to Shine

PART 1
From Precious to Indispensable
Silver Matters Now More Than Ever

An Insider's View of The Silver Market

Silver is the future—and I've been sounding the alarm for years.

In every interview, article, or conversation with anyone willing to listen, I've made it clear that you need to hold silver in your investment portfolio.

Aside from its investing aspect, silver's industrial applications will drive demand and increase prices.

The more I reflected on silver's future, the more I came to realize:

SILVER IS THE NEW OIL

Silver is positioned similarly to oil in the late 1800s when oil transitioned from a relatively obscure commodity to a driving force of industrial growth and economic power.

Silver will become a significant wealth and opportunity generator, similar to how oil became a critical and highly valuable resource after gaining mass adoption.

Silver is more than a precious metal. It is a vital industrial commodity. As its use expands and evolves, it becomes essential and significantly more valuable.

Silver will mirror oil in 3 ways:

1. It's opportunity.
2. It will fuel the future of energy.
3. It will be all around us and incorporated into everyday products we rely on.

I will lay out the facts and show you the opportunities investors need to recognize.

Let's start with the basics: **Why Silver?**

Because of these driving factors:

Industrial Demand: Silver's unmatched conductivity and reflectivity make it essential in high-tech industries.

Economic Hedge: A proven protector against inflation and currency devaluation.

Supply Constraints: Global reserves are depleting, and mining output lags behind surging demand—a setup for price appreciation.

Investment Accessibility: More affordable than gold, making it accessible to a broader range of investors with substantial upside potential.

All precious metals have inherent value, but when it comes to silver, technological innovations and advances mean that each discovery establishes another demand source.

As much as I love gold, silver is indispensable in our modern world.

SECRET SILVER
Antidote for Mercury Poisoning
Silver chloride isn't just a compound; it's a lifesaver! Used to treat mercury poisoning, it helps flush deadly toxins from the body, showcasing silver's protective health benefits.

My Mission

I want to inspire you to take action.

I want to show you how you can generate outsized, asymmetrical returns by positioning yourself today ahead of those who chase opportunity.

I've helped my clients prosper, as well as built and maintained my wealth by asking one question:

What's next?

Over the past two decades, I have studied and worked alongside numerous millionaires. I can tell you that the most straightforward and explosive wealth creation I've witnessed comes from moments—tiny windows of opportunity.

Transitionary periods.

Unlike Jerome Powell's 'transitory inflation,' these wealth-building moments come and go quickly. Blink, and you'll miss your opportunity.

So, when these windows open, you must pounce—move quickly without hesitating or second-guessing yourself.

You can only move like that if you are prepared and stalking the opportunity.

The problem is that most people need help to spot these moments of change.

Sure, they see change in hindsight.

But we can't invest in the past.

Don't go through life being the person who says things like:

"I had the idea for that app years ago but never made it."

"I should've invested in Tesla before it skyrocketed."

"I knew that house was a good deal. I should've made an offer."

The reality is that most people cannot look to the future, analyze where they are heading, and take advantage of opportunities.

Most people fail to notice change.

Most people are too wrapped up in their reality to notice everything shifting around them.

I wrote this book because I want you to prosper.

I want to eliminate your excuses.

You deserve to live the life of your dreams. If you've failed to capitalize on previous opportunities, I can point you in the right direction.

This book is your compass.

I'm telling you: **We're entering one of those magical transformative times.**

A seismic shift is coming —

To prosper, you must prepare.

We are on the cusp of a transition that will push us so far forward into a new reality that we will NEVER return to this moment — like when color TV killed black & white TV. We aren't coming back to this moment ever again.

The revolution in the silver market will be driven by cutting-edge technological advancements, propelling our society forward.

If you are currently not invested or under-invested in silver, then you most likely fall into one of two groups:

One: You don't see the opportunity and are unaware of it.

OR

Two: You see it but don't know how to capitalize on it.

I will guide both groups across the bridge from inaction to action.

Because if you hesitate, you will miss another opportunity to secure your financial future.

History has shown you can not wait until something IS happening to act.

Those who benefit do so because they capitalize on the things no one else sees coming and take action IMMEDIATELY.

Your future is based solely on your decisions and actions you take today.

What I see now, and you will soon realize, is that:

Silver and Oil Are More Alike Than You Realize

OIL vs. SILVER	
Versatility & Industrial	
Oil is a versatile energy resource with widespread applications beyond fuel. It is a critical ingredient in producing plastics, chemicals, lubricants, and various industrial products. The petrochemical industry relies heavily on oil derivatives for manufacturing.	Silver is highly versatile and used in numerous industrial applications. It is crucial in electronics, solar panels, medical devices, and countless other technologies. Its unique properties, including conductivity and reflectivity, make it indispensable in many industries.
Technology & Innovation	
Oil is a fundamental resource for technological advancement. It powers transportation, supports manufacturing processes, and serves as a raw material for producing a wide range of products, from synthetic materials to pharmaceuticals.	Silver plays a pivotal role in technological innovation. It is essential for producing electronic components, conductive links, and nanotechnological advancements. Silver's contribution to emerging technologies positions it as a driver of innovation.

OIL vs. SILVER	
Healthcare & Medical	
"Much of the medical equipment used today, many of which are life-saving devices, is made from oil. Not only are heart valves and artificial limbs made from petroleum, but also many of the cleaning and safety products medical personnel use. Aspirins and other pharmaceuticals also contain petroleum."[1]	"Today's scientists pay great attention to silver, although its preparations have been used for wound healing ever since ancient times. Among metals, silver is particularly widely used in medicine and has a well-documented antimicrobial effect against Gram-positive and Gram-negative bacteria, fungi, protozoa and viruses."[2]
Investment & Commodities	
Oil is a major global commodity and is actively traded on international markets. It is an essential component of national economies and a focus of geopolitical considerations.	Investors consider silver a precious metal and use it for investment purposes. Traders exchange silver on commodity markets, and many see it as a store of value.
Energy	
Oil has historically been the world's primary energy source, enabling transportation, electricity, and industrial processes as a dense hydrocarbon fuel.	Silver is a critical component in solar panels, contributing to the growth of renewable energy sources. Its conductivity enhances the efficiency of solar cells.

---

1 https://www.iogp.org/blog/news/uses-of-oil-and-gas-in-the-medical-field/
2 https://www.ncbi.nlm.nih.gov/pmc/articles/PMC10650883/#:~:text=Among%20
    metals%2C%20silver%20is%20particularly,viruses%20%5B16%2C17%5D.

THE WEALTH WINDOW IS OPEN

Silver isn't just a metal—it's your key to financial freedom.

A gateway to wealth.

Will you step through it or let it pass?

The choice will shape your legacy.

PART 2
A 21st Century Industrial Revolution

The Opportunity

Throughout my career, I have only seen a handful of moments as ripe with opportunity as the one before us.

For over a century, oil has powered the world's engine, but as the world races toward renewable energy, this engine is on the brink of transformation.

SECRET SILVER
Hip Implants*

Silver coats the bearings in some hip joint implants. This groundbreaking technology not only wards off infections but also utilizes silver's self-lubrication properties, enhancing the longevity and durability of implants while improving patients' lives and mobility.

*Having recently undergone a hip replacement, I've gained an appreciation for these advances in medical technology. These innovations aid post-op healing, significantly improve recovery, and help protect patients from infections. As someone on the younger side of the hip replacement spectrum due to college athletic injuries, I particularly appreciate these developments and the long-term health benefits they provide.

The push for renewable energy will thrust silver into the spotlight, positioning it as the most in-demand commodity in the world.

This shift won't just alter our energy landscape—it's a market upheaval set to disrupt the delicate balance of silver's supply and demand, driving prices sharply upward.

As of this writing, silver's price is approximately $30 per ounce.

Based on my research, I foresee a short-term price target of $48 and a longer-term target of $60 per ounce. In fact, looking at how the market is shaping up, $60 might underestimate the opportunity.

Doubling in price from today's levels might be the first leg of a much larger, longer push.

How many times in your life do you get the chance to double every dollar you invest?

This isn't hype or wishful thinking—it's reality.

We are on the cusp of a technological revolution that will require a steady supply of silver.

Silver is vital to the evolution of 21st-century technologies, and research shows that our current reserves are insufficient to meet the demand necessary for transitioning to a world reliant on renewable energy.

How Much Silver Is Needed for the United States to Go Completely Solar?

To estimate how much silver it would take for the United States to generate all its electricity from solar power, we need to start with some key numbers.

1. **Annual Electricity Consumption:** In 2023, "Electricity consumption in the United States totaled 4,000 terawatt-hours(TWh)."[3] This translates to approximately 11 terawatt-hours (TWh) per day.
2. **Power Output of Solar Panels:** "solar panels will produce about 2 kilowatt-hours (kWh) of electricity daily."[4]
3. **Silver Content in Solar Panels:** "The average solar panel contains 0.643 ounces (20 grams) of silver."[5]

Using these figures, let's break down the calculations:

Step 1: Calculate the Number of Panels Needed

To generate 11 terawatt-hours (TWh) per day using solar power:

- **1 terawatt-hour (TWh)** is equal to **1 billion kilowatt-hours (kWh).**
- **11 TWh** is, therefore, equivalent to **11 billion kWh** of electricity daily.

---

3 https://www.statista.com/statistics/201794/us-electricity-consumption-since-1975/#:~:text=Electricity%20consumption%20in%20the%20United,increasing%20in%20the%20next%20decades.
4 https://www.solarreviews.com/blog/how-much-electricity-does-a-solar-panel-produce
5 https://boabmetals.com/blog/solar-energy-powering-silver-demand/

Given that each solar panel produces **2 kWh** of electricity per day, we would need:

$$\frac{11 \text{ billion kWh}}{2 \text{ kWh per panel}} = 5.5 \text{ billion solar panels}$$

Step 2: Calculate the Amount of Silver Required

Each solar panel contains **0.643 ounces** of silver. So, if we need **5.5 billion solar panels**, the total silver required would be:

$$5.5 \text{ billion panels} \times 0.643 \text{ ounces per panel} = 3.5365 \text{ billion ounces of silver}$$

We would need 3.5365 billion ounces of silver

Step 3: Compare with Total Silver Ever Mined

To put this in perspective:

- "The total amount of silver ever mined is approximately **55.94 billion ounces.**"[6]
- Global silver production in 2023 was "**831 million ounces (Moz).**"[7]

If the U.S. were to build enough solar infrastructure to power the country entirely on solar energy, the project would require about **3.54 billion ounces of silver**—or **about 6.3%** of all the silver ever mined.

With current global production levels at around 831 million ounces annually, such a project would require

---

6   https://www.bullionbypost.co.uk/index/silver/amount-of-silver-in-the-world/#:~:text=It%20
    is%20estimated%20that%2C%20by,stored%20as%20investment%20silver%20bullion.
7   https://www.jpost.com/business-and-innovation/precious-metals/article-812788

over **four years' worth of the entire world's silver production** solely for U.S. solar needs.

Is It Feasible?

The sheer scale of silver required to fully transition the U.S. to solar energy places unprecedented demands on global silver resources. This would require years of worldwide production and could drive prices higher, underscoring the challenge of meeting such ambitious goals with current silver supply and mining capabilities.

It's such a concern that some experts warn all the silver ever mined could be depleted within the next 20 years.

This is our opportunity.

"Silver Mines Will Likely Be Bought By Automakers Like Tesla... Silver To $125 Per Ounce"

- KEITH NEUMEYER

Demand for silver is expanding as new applications emerge, and the quantity needed continues to rise.

YET SUPPLY REMAINS LIMITED AND TIGHTLY CONSTRAINED.

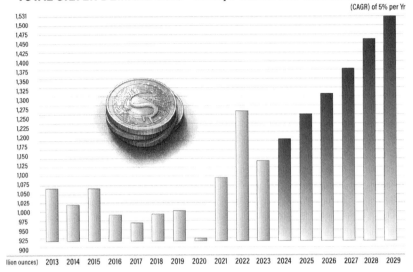

TOTAL SILVER DEMAND 2013 - 2023; PROJECTED THROUGH 2029

(CAGR) of 5% per Yr

In fact, the silver market has been in deficit for the past few years.

While manageable until now, this shortfall will become glaring as demand intensifies—and this is the market dynamic we, as silver investors, are going to exploit.

Every investor, entrepreneur, and business owner understands the fundamentals of supply and demand, which is why I'm so confident—and excited—about this opportunity.

Look at the size of the silver market compared to oil:

How Big is the Silver Market Compared to the Oil Market ?

$2.1 TRILLION CRUDE OIL MARKET   **$20 BILLION SILVER MARKET**

Market sizes are calculated by multiplying annual production in 2022 with spot prices as of June 7, 2023

Imagine silver's market value expanding to match that of oil.

Silver's Supply and Demand

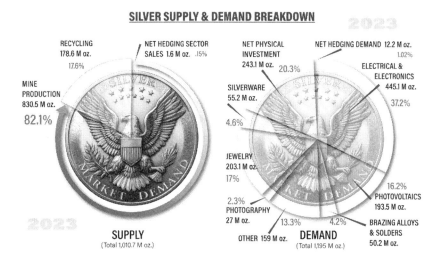

SILVER SUPPLY & DEMAND BREAKDOWN 2023

RECYCLING 178.6 M oz. 17.6%

NET HEDGING SECTOR SALES 1.6 M oz. .15%

MINE PRODUCTION 830.5 M oz. 82.1%

SUPPLY (Total 1,010.7 M oz.)

NET PHYSICAL INVESTMENT 243.1 M oz. 20.3%

NET HEDGING DEMAND 12.2 M oz. 1.02%

ELECTRICAL & ELECTRONICS 445.1 M oz. 37.2%

SILVERWARE 55.2 M oz. 4.6%

JEWELRY 203.1 M oz. 17%

16.2% PHOTOVOLTAICS 193.5 M oz.

2.3% PHOTOGRAPHY 27 M oz.

13.3% OTHER 159 M oz.

4.2% BRAZING ALLOYS & SOLDERS 50.2 M oz.

DEMAND (Total 1,195 M oz.)

It's Economics 101: as demand rises, one of two things **MUST** increase—supply or price.

Supply and demand operate like a seesaw.

SUPPLY   DEMAND

Supply: The quantity sellers are willing to offer.
Demand: The quantity buyers are ready to purchase.

If supply is high but demand is low, prices drop to encourage more purchases—imagine a cafeteria full of pizzas but only a few hungry students; the price would naturally drop.

On the other hand, when demand outpaces supply, prices climb; if everyone wants pizza and only a few are available, prices will rise to balance the demand.

Balancing Act

The seesaw continuously seeks balance.

When supply rises but demand remains steady, prices fall to restore equilibrium.

When demand rises but supply remains steady, prices increase to achieve balance.

This "equilibrium price" is the point where supply and demand are balanced.

The Shift to a New Equilibrium

As a macroeconomic investor, I foresee an upward shift in silver's equilibrium price, driven by rising demand coupled with a steady or declining supply.

Once an imbalance is triggered—when the price moves from balance to imbalance— it's challenging for prices to revert to their equilibrium price.

Equilibrium price finds a new balance point that is rarely at its previous level.

Today, silver is evolving from its traditional role as a precious metal to a critical component in modern industry, marking a turning point in global resource dynamics.

Silver is now powering advancements in solar energy, electronics, and clean water technology. With silver's industrial applications expanding, economic projections predict a widening gap between demand and supply over the coming decade.

Silver to Remain in Deep Deficit

(Annual Supply Minus Demand, in millions of ounces)

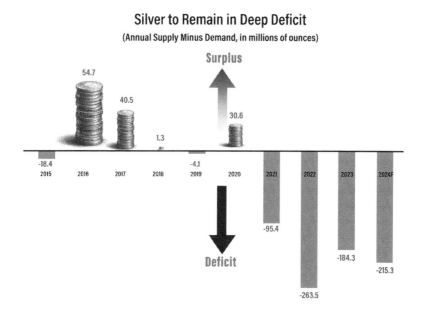

A New Era of Silver Shortages?

I envision a world where we experience silver shortages that could mirror the oil shortages of past decades. Headlines are already raising concerns.

There are reports that the "Supply of New Silver is Drying Up Quicker Than Death Valley" and "The lack of new silver discoveries almost guarantees a supply squeeze soon. The rush to secure more silver is creating excitement."[8]

Other reports share that sentiment:

"Global Silver Industrial Demand Forecast to Achieve New High in 2023."[9]

"Silver Industrial demand is expected to grow 8% to a record 632 million ounces (Moz) this year."

"Important Silver Demand Drivers to Effectively Double Rate of Growth Over Next Decade."[10]

"New research indicates that silver industrial demand is forecast to increase 46 percent through 2033, while jewelry and silverware demand is projected to rise 34 and 30 percent."[11]

8   https://newsdirect.com/news/
    ev-demand-could-have-a-major-effect-on-the-price-of-silver-590610436
9   global-silver-industrial-demand-forecast-to.pdf
10 https://www.globenewswire.com/news-release/2023/11/08/2776467/0/en/Important-
    Silver-Demand-Drivers-to-Effectively-Double-Rate-of-Growth-Over-Next-Decade.html
11 https://www.globenewswire.com/news-release/2023/11/08/2776467/0/en/Important-
    Silver-Demand-Drivers-to-Effectively-Double-Rate-of-Growth-Over-Next-Decade.html

The need for silver is NOT SLOWING DOWN.

Silver Demand

Demand (million) oz.	2015	2016	2017	2018	2019	2020	2021	2022	2023	2024F	2023	2024
Industrial (total)											11%	9%
Electrical & Electronics											20%	9%
...of which photovoltaics											64%	20%
Brazing Alloys & Solders											2%	3%
Other Industrial											-5%	9%
Photography											-2%	-3%
Jewelry											-13%	4%
Silverware											-25%	7%
Net Physical Investment											-28%	-13%
Net Hedging Demand											-32%	na
Total Demand (Million ounces)	1,065.4	861.8	971.8	999.2	1,004.4	926.8	1,099.6	1,278.9	1,195.0	1,219.1	-7%	2%

Statistics in this section were adapted in part from the Silver Institute's World Silver Survey 2024.

Silver is Irreplaceable

As silver becomes increasingly valuable, you might wonder, "Can we substitute silver with another material?"

While substitution is common in other sectors when prices rise, silver's unique properties make it irreplaceable. Few materials match its combination of electrical conductivity, thermal stability, and durability. Replacing silver would compromise the efficiency, safety, and effectiveness of cutting-edge technologies.

As cheaper alternatives fall short, silver's demand will remain robust, even with rising prices and limited supply.

When it comes to precious metals, one thing is clear: Silver Reigns Supreme.

Silver Reigns Supreme

Silver sits at the center of numerous industries and offers unique advantages across diverse sectors.

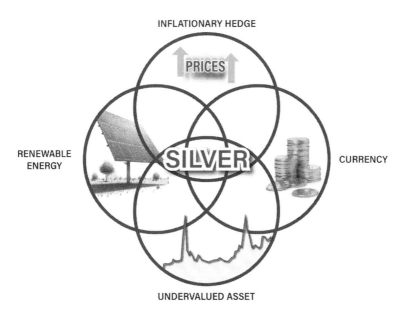

- **Portfolio Diversification:** Silver's low correlation with traditional financial assets makes it a standout choice for portfolio diversification. Its performance often moves independently from other investments, adding resilience to portfolios.

- **Hedging Against Inflation:** Silver has a proven track record as a hedge against inflation, with prices soaring during the inflationary periods of the 1970s and early 1980s. This history makes it a go-to for investors looking to preserve purchasing power and safeguard portfolios during times of rising prices.
- **Safe-Haven Asset:** During economic uncertainty or geopolitical instability, silver shines as a safe-haven asset. Its reliable store of value makes it an appealing choice for investors seeking security in volatile times.
- **Intrinsic Value:** Silver's intrinsic value is rooted in its rarity, durability, and extensive utility. Unlike many financial assets, it carries inherent worth.
- **Industrial Demand:** Silver's extensive industrial use sets it apart from other precious metals. It's critical in the electronics, medical, and renewable energy sectors. This dual demand—from investors seeking a store of value and industries relying on its unique properties—truly distinguishes silver from gold.

Chart the Course

I'm not a technical trader, but I want to share an intriguing silver chart that captures silver's long-term potential.

This chart uses a 12-month, or yearly, candle format, where each bar represents a full year of silver price movement in a single visual element.

Here's how to read each candle:

- **The length of the bar** shows the year's price range, from the lowest price (bottom) to the highest price (top).
- **The thick part of the bar, or 'body,'** represents opening and closing prices:
  - ▶ If the body is hollow, the closing price is higher than the opening price.
  - ▶ If the body is red, the closing price is lower than the opening.
- **Wicks** are thin lines extending from the body, indicating the highest and lowest prices during the year.

This yearly view provides a clear picture of long-term trends and volatility in silver.

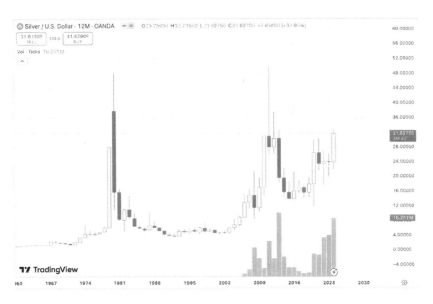

What stands out to me is that silver has previously hit highs around $50/oz twice: once in the early 1980s at $48.00 and again in the early 2000s at $49.80.

This indicates that prices have previously reached the $50 mark, suggesting a clear path for them to return to that level.

When I look at this chart, I see waves of investor emotions: traders chasing price action and latecomers pushing prices to unsustainable highs.

This cycle will likely repeat.

Here's how it typically plays out:

Early investors begin the movement, pushing prices up gradually.

Momentum builds as more traders buy in, fueling the upward trend.

Breakout traders watch for the $50 mark, and as it breaks, they fuel a rapid price increase.

Latecomers join in, driven by excitement and greed, pushing prices to euphoric heights—this frenzy can provide the fuel to send silver prices to uncharted territory.

Once this silver trade gains momentum, it will move fast and climb higher than anyone can predict.

This is how I established my short- and mid-term targets. Silver at $48/oz feels like a given, and $60 on momentum alone is within reach. The real thrill lies in what could follow. Could silver hit $75 as excitement peaks and speculators drive prices beyond fundamentals? I think so.

SECRET SILVER
Wood Preservative
Preserve your wood structures with silver! Silver acts as a highly effective biocide, preventing decay and deterring termites to keep wood durable and pristine.

We've seen asset bubbles before, and human nature hasn't changed—investors are drawn to stories and the thrill of chasing price action.

But instead of chasing, we'll already be positioned and ready.

Be First

Everyone who misses a trade, trend, or opportunity always has the same sob story:

I WISH I knew about that sooner...
I WISH I could go back and invest...
I WISH I'd listened to that advice...

I'm sharing this information with you so you won't have to utter those words as you watch silver prices skyrocket.

I want you to get involved BEFORE the train leaves the station.

In financial opportunities, you're either in or out.

You invest, or you don't.

That's it.

The truth is most Americans need help understanding what's happening. They live with their heads down, hoping success and wealth will find them.

Unfortunately, success and wealth often pass by those types of people.

Even when someone offers them a chance, they miss it. They're too distracted to recognize opportunities and, as a result, fail to act.

That's not you. **You bought this book because you're ready to take action**. You're ready to build a better, more secure future.

Silver is our opportunity to be like Colonel Drake, who struck oil in Pennsylvania in 1859, or to be among the early investors at Texas's legendary Spindletop oil discovery in 1901.

We can own a commodity on the launching pad, ready to take off.

As the world grapples with the consequences of climate change and the finite nature of fossil fuels, they will NEED to embrace sustainable alternatives.

As the world turns from fossil fuels to sustainable energy, it will **need** silver to power these technologies.

We will own the metal that enables all renewable energy technologies.

You can't produce these technologies without silver.

And right now is the best time to build your position.

I suspect institutional investors are already accumulating significant silver positions.

You may wonder, *"Why haven't I heard about silver in the news?"*

No investor is going to broadcast silver's rising demand and limited supply while they're quietly building their position.

Accumulation is silent.

The beauty of silver is that we can get into the same trade as the "smart money"—without raising prices or disrupting the opportunity.

Now is the time to enter, while supply and demand are still balanced. Don't wait for the imbalance to hit. Position yourself to benefit from the initial price surge and start building profit early.

DID YOU KNOW:
An ounce of silver can be drawn into a strand of wire 8,000 feet long.

ALL THE SILVER EVER MINED WOULD FIT IN A CUBE 55 METERS ON EACH SIDE

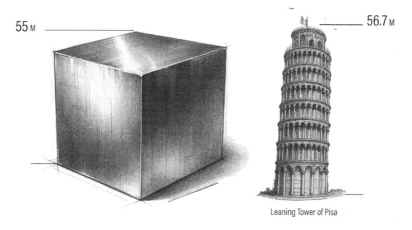

55 M

56.7 M

Leaning Tower of Pisa

One of my researchers shared a compelling insight with me after six months of working on this book:

She said, "We're on the verge of a Silver Supercycle."

What is a Supercycle?

"A supercycle is a prolonged period of strong economic growth, leading to sustained demand for commodities beyond what producers can supply. Supercycles can last years."[12]

---

12   https://corporatefinanceinstitute.com/resources/economics/supercycle/

These extended periods of imbalance create exceptional opportunities for investors to profit from rising prices and the increasing value of essential commodities.

As silver becomes increasingly rare, new millionaires will be minted.

Will you be one of them?

Are you ready to act and take steps to secure your position now?

OR

Will you pass on this investment and then look back in ten years and play the "what if game?"

I've highlighted the opportunity for you: the growing imbalance in silver's supply and demand.

In the next section, I'll explain why this imbalance is coming—and why transitioning to a new essential resource is the chance of a lifetime.

SECRET SILVER
NASA's Water Purification
NASA employed innovative uses of silver ions for water purification aboard the Apollo spacecraft. This lightweight and effective method ditched traditional chlorine for silver ions, ensuring astronauts had access to bacteria-free water.

PART 3
Fueling the Post-Oil Economy

Oil Runs the World

Oil has fundamentally shaped the world we know today, influencing everything from foreign policy to economic stability. Nations wield oil as a weapon, leveraging it to manipulate economies, shape alliances, and, at times, ignite conflicts.

DID YOU KNOW:
With less than 5% of the world's population, the U.S. consumes 16% of the world's energy[13]

This dependency has compelled countries, particularly the United States, to navigate complex geopolitical landscapes and forge strategic alliances to secure this vital resource.

While oil has been a cornerstone of economic growth, it has also locked the U.S. into complex and volatile global relationships.

But now is the time to reevaluate our reliance on this volatile commodity.

We stand on the brink of the next industrial revolution: **The Shift to Sustainability**.

---

13   https://css.umich.edu/publications/factsheets/energy/us-energy-system-factsheet

This transition is more than a shift in commodities. It's an evolution toward sustainable practices, technological innovation, and a reimagining of economic and global interdependencies.

Why is it essential to redefine our energy dependency?

As Ari Shapiro reported on All Things Considered in February 2023,

"Russia's war in Ukraine has implications far beyond the battlefield, including energy. The flow of oil, natural gas, and refined products like diesel has been upended, leading to one of the largest shifts in the global energy market in decades."[14]

When you control the flow of energy, you hold power.

The fact that one nation can disrupt another's energy supply at will underscores the urgency of achieving energy independence.

The smooth operation of America's energy grid hinges on foreign oil, underscoring the need to achieve energy independence and shift away from external suppliers.

Before we discuss how to reduce our reliance on foreign oil, let's examine how we arrived at this pivotal point.

---

14   https://www.npr.org/2023/02/28/1160157753/how-russias-war-in-ukraine-is-changing-the-worlds-oil-markets

United States' Dependence On Oil

The United States' reliance on oil began with the Industrial Revolution, a transformative era marked by rapid industrialization and the widespread adoption of oil.

As the nation progressed, oil became more than just a fuel—it became the lifeblood of American industry and daily life.

Oil's unmatched energy efficiency solidified it as the foundation of transportation and a cornerstone of the economy and society.

Economic growth and prosperity quickly drove the United States to embrace the automobile, reinforcing the nation's dependence on oil. For Americans, cars became symbols of freedom and mobility, fueling widespread adoption and increasing oil demand.

SECRET SILVER
Antifreeze
Next time you top up your car's coolant, think of silver! Silver is used indirectly as a catalyst in producing ethylene glycol and plays an indirect but crucial role in antifreeze production, helping engines run smoothly in all climates.

As the Industrial Revolution advanced, oil demand surged again with the rise of aviation and maritime transport, now vital to global commerce and travel.

Throughout the 20th century, America's dependence on oil deepened, transforming it from a convenient resource to the backbone of modern life.

In the 1970s, after abandoning the gold standard (see "The Gold Standard" on page 61), the United States became even more intertwined with oil with the establishment of the petro-dollar agreement. President Nixon agreed with Saudi Arabia and other OPEC nations to stabilize the U.S. dollar, guaranteeing that all oil would be priced and traded exclusively in U.S. dollars.

In exchange for pricing their oil exports in U.S. dollars, these countries received military protection, weapons sales, and other economic incentives from the United States.

This agreement created an enduring economic bond and deepened U.S. military and geopolitical commitments with oil-exporting nations. Despite inherent trade-offs and complexities, the deal reinforced the dollar's global dominance and expanded America's influence.

The arrangement also ensured that any nation wanting to buy oil on the global market would need to hold U.S. dollars, creating a continuous demand for the currency and reinforcing the dollar as the world's primary reserve currency.

This petrodollar system secured the U.S.'s position in global finance and offered strategic benefits to participating oil-exporting countries. However, the inclusion of military support and weapons sales added layers of complexity to the agreement, requiring the U.S. to navigate relationships with volatile regions. At the time, it was a necessary trade-off viewed as a strategic win-win for all parties involved.

THE GOLD STANDARD

The gold standard is a system where the value of a country's currency is linked to a certain amount of gold. This means the government promises to exchange its money for gold at a fixed price whenever requested.

While on the gold standard, fiat money functions like gold because it's always exchangeable at a guaranteed rate.

There's a reason J.P. Morgan said, 'Gold is money. Everything else is credit.'

The United States was on the gold standard until 1971, when President Nixon abandoned it and decoupled the U.S. dollar from gold.

Why?

Three main reasons:

Economic Pressure

In the late 1960s and early 1970s, the United States faced many economic problems, including high inflation and large trade deficits, which put pressure on the dollar.

Demand for Gold

Under the Bretton Woods system, countries settled international balances in U.S. dollars, which were convertible to gold at a fixed rate of $35 an ounce. The United States maintained this fixed gold price and adjusted the dollar supply to ensure confidence in future gold convertibility.

However, persistent U.S. balance-of-payments deficits led to a critical situation. Countries like France and others began losing confidence in the dollar's stability. As foreign-held dollars started to exceed the U.S. gold stock, these nations increasingly requested to exchange their dollars for gold, fearing the U.S. might be unable to fulfill its obligation to redeem dollars at the official gold price.

This trend caused a rapid decrease in U.S. gold reserves, putting the country at risk of depleting its gold stockpile. The mounting pressure on U.S. gold reserves highlighted the unsustainability of the system.[15]

Maintaining Economic Stability

The U.S. and global economies had grown to the point where there wasn't enough gold to cover all the money in circulation.

On August 15, 1971, President Nixon announced a series of economic measures in a plan known as the Nixon Shock.

The most significant was closing the "gold window," which meant that the U.S. would no longer allow dollars to be exchanged for gold at a fixed price. This decision effectively ended the gold standard.

What Happened?

After Nixon removed the U.S. from the gold standard, our currency began to have floating exchange rates, which means their values could change based on market conditions like supply and demand in foreign exchange markets.

The U.S. government also gained more flexibility in controlling its money supply and interest rates, which allowed it to better manage the economy.

The removal of the gold standard changed the dynamics of our financial system and caused volatility in global markets.

---

15   https://www.federalreservehistory.org/essays/bretton-woods-created#:~:text=Countries%20 settled%20international%20balances%20in,the%20dollar's%20convertibility%20to%20gold.

The petrodollar deal was struck to reduce the volatility and maintain the dollar's dominance.

Isn't it interesting that the petrodollar system was established in 1973 after Nixon took the United States off the gold standard, which caused extreme volatility in the dollar and sent shockwaves through the economic system?

The end of the gold standard marked a transformative era in global finance, setting the stage for a world of fiat currencies and complex international currency dependencies.

Thanks to Nixon and all the political jockeying, we had oil and a stable dollar.

This interdependence came with vulnerabilities, linking America's interests to politically volatile nations. Present-day conflicts, such as the one between Israel and Hamas, demonstrate how distant events can impact the United States. Since the conflict began, the U.S. has heightened efforts to protect oil-dominated shipping lanes in the area.

ABC News recently reported, "The U.S. Navy has been in the region for decades, but the Navy and Coast Guard's mission to protect shipping lanes and international commerce, in light of the described threats, is a relatively recent one."[16]

This raises an interesting question: How much money does America spend protecting oil?

As of 2018, Vox reported, "The U.S. military spends a minimum of $81 billion a year protecting oil supplies."[17]

---

16   https://abcnews.go.com/International/
     red-sea-shipping-lanes-under-attack-israel-hamas-war-analysis/story?id=105416850
17   https://www.vox.com/energy-and-environment/2018/9/21/17885832/
     oil-subsidies-military-protection-supplies-safe

Their estimated figure is "16 percent of the Department of Defense's base annual budget" in 2018.

Some analysts speculate that "approximately 16 percent of the defense budget is dedicated to protecting global oil interests"[18]

In 2023, our defense budget was $857.9 billion.[19]

16% is over $137 billion!

SECRET SILVER
Silver-Oxide Batteries
These tiny but powerful batteries boast 40% more runtime than traditional lithium-ion, and the fact that devices like hearing aids and watches use them, these batteries are powering our everyday gadgets.

America needs to reassess its place in the energy landscape. Setting politics aside, it's clear we must shift toward renewable energy.

This transition to renewables is not only about the environment but is also strategic as we navigate the complexities of the 21st century and our national security.

In today's geopolitical landscape, energy remains the backbone of modern economies, and securing dominance in this area is vital to maintaining both economic power and global influence.

Failure to prioritize domestic energy would leave the U.S. reliant on foreign oil, risking economic control by countries that dictate the price of oil and gas exports.

We cannot remain politically vulnerable, forced into action due to our reliance on foreign resources to maintain our lifestyle.

---

18 https://www.climatejusticecenter.org/newsletter/the-toxic-relationship-between-oil-and-the-military
19 https://www.armed-services.senate.gov/imo/media/doc/fy23_ndaa_agreement_summary.pdf

This vulnerability is evident in our reliance on Middle Eastern oil and relations with nations like Russia. We must reclaim our energy future through sustainable domestic industries and innovative technologies.

By controlling our own energy supply, we can reset international relationships, gaining independence and freedom.

The United States now stands at a pivotal juncture, facing a hard decision: Embrace a new energy revolution or remain dependent on unstable foreign resources.

To stay a superpower, America must achieve energy independence by leading in the development and production of renewable energy. Doing so will solidify our status as a global powerhouse by controlling our own energy resources, reducing reliance on foreign oil, and securing economic resilience for future generations.

I've said this before, and I'll say it again because it's at the core of my message:

The next superpower will be the country that dominates energy. Our dependence on oil makes us dependent on the Middle East. To remain a global superpower, we must achieve energy independence by leading in the transition to renewable energy technology and production.

Yes, oil is dirty and causes environmental damage.

Yes, we need to reduce our carbon footprint.

SECRET SILVER
Stained Glass
Did you know you can transform ordinary glass into stained glass with silver nitrate? Silver nitrate penetrates the glass and infuses it with shades from light yellow to deep amber, adding a touch of historical craftsmanship to modern artistry.

Yes, our reliance on fossil fuels is unsustainable in the long term.

But above all, we must adapt now to control the technologies that will shape our future.

The Key To Retaining The U.S. Global Economic Dominance

When I try to predict the future of our economy and global standing, it's clear both are at risk.

Globalization has shrunk the world, and as a nation, we're no longer the unstoppable juggernaut we once were.

Some countries have been relentlessly trying to dethrone us, and these threats need to be taken seriously.

I can't help but think of two sayings:

"The enemy of my enemy is my friend."
"The whole is greater than the sum of its parts."

These quotes capture the shifting alliances that jeopardize U.S. dominance. Nations once divided are now uniting against us, forming powerful alliances.

Aggressive foreign policies and short-sighted economic strategies have fostered adversaries worldwide.

Believing we were too large and untouchable, we pushed our agenda onto other countries without considering the long-term consequences. This arrogance fueled resentment and opposition, leading to a growing number of adversaries eager to challenge our position on the global stage.

As the world has grown smaller and technology has enabled more transparent communication, smaller countries have been able to form powerful alliances.

What were once small, individual economies and countries with limited power have now transformed into dynamic unions and agreements that circumvent our influence and control.

America has worked itself into a precarious position.

It's like in the movies where the bully is strong one-on-one, but when everyone he's picked on bands together, he suddenly finds himself at a disadvantage.

Let's take a look at the recent development with BRICS.

BRICS is the acronym for a group of rising powers—Brazil, Russia, India, China, and South Africa—whose economies and geopolitical ambitions must now be reckoned with on the world stage.

BRICS: Brazil · Russia · India · China · South Africa

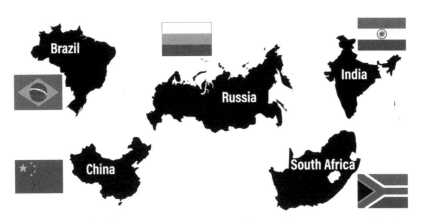

A key goal of BRICS is to create a shared currency, reducing their reliance on the U.S. dollar and increasing economic independence.

This currency would likely be backed by gold, providing stability and value.

If these countries successfully form such a currency, it would significantly threaten the American dollar's dominance in global markets.

Such a currency would reduce these nations' reliance on the dollar, effectively diminishing U.S. leverage and challenging our global influence.

How would their new monetary system affect ours?

The goal of the BRICS currency is to allow them to bypass our dollar and transact in a stable intermediary currency.

Nixon established the petrodollar system to stabilize the dollar by linking it to the oil trade, creating a steady demand for U.S. currency. Now, that stability could be slipping away. Without the petrodollar's anchoring effect, global financial dynamics may shift dramatically, raising serious questions about U.S. economic security.

Is the Petrodollar Dying?

The dominance of the petrodollar is under increasing pressure.

The *Wall Street Journal* recently reported, "Saudi Arabia is in active talks with Beijing to price some of its oil sales to China in yuan...a move that would dent the U.S. dollar's dominance of the global petroleum market."[20]

An article from the Atlantic Council also stated, "Saudi Arabia's willingness to diversify the currencies used in selling its oil aligns with a larger strategy that requires the country to increase its international relations beyond the United States."[21] The article adds, "Saudi Arabia's

---

20 https://www.wsj.com/articles/saudi-arabia-considers-accepting-yuan-instead-of-dollars-for-chinese-oil-sales-11647351541

21 https://www.atlanticcouncil.org/blogs/econographics/is-the-end-of-the-petrodollar-near/

interest in currency diversification marks a small but symbolic step down the road toward de-dollarization."[22]

Whether the petrodollar agreement collapses or is significantly modified, this shift signals a major red flag for U.S. entanglement in the global oil economy. The growing movement toward de-dollarization could point to a long-term transition away from the petrodollar system, potentially leading to a gradual decline in U.S. economic influence over the coming years.

Bloomberg pointed out that "the expansion of the BRICS group could pave the way for a more multifaceted and less dollar-centric global oil market."[23]

So, not only is depleting the natural supply of oil usage a significant concern, but the stability surrounding the oil economy is at risk.

A recurring theme in all our international conflicts and policies is our dependence on oil and deep involvement in the global oil economy.

Our dependence on oil also makes us dependent on other countries and forces us to form relationships that complicate our international policies.

The Russian invasion of Ukraine should have been a wake-up call for the U.S. to accelerate energy independence and secure our economic future. We can no longer leave our economic well-being tied to other countries.

The message is clear: the U.S. must move from oil dependence to sustainable energy to secure its future, reduce its

---

22 https://www.atlanticcouncil.org/blogs/econographics/is-the-end-of-the-petrodollar-near/
23 https://www.bloomberg.com/professional/blog/larger-brics-to-dominate-oil-pricing/#:~:
    text=In%20essence%2C%20the%20expansion%20of,is%20
    a%20trend%20worth%20monitoring.

entanglements in global conflicts, and reclaim control over its economy.

History proves that superpowers thrive when they control their own resources. For the U.S. to preserve its leadership, energy independence is no longer an option—it's a necessity.

Examining how past empires leveraged essential resources to maintain dominance highlights what's at stake for the U.S. today: achieving true independence and securing our leadership on the world stage.

Securing our future, maintaining leadership, and embracing energy independence aren't just goals—they're imperatives for America's continued strength.

Empires That Dominate Resources Dominate The World

History shows, time and again, that control over vital resources equates to global dominance. This fundamental truth has shaped civilizations, driven conquests, and determined global power structures for millennia.

Let's examine some of history's most powerful empires, focusing on the essential resources that propelled their ascent, maintained their supremacy, and ultimately contributed to their decline:

Roman Empire (27 BC – 476 AD)

- Grain
- Precious metals
- Stone
- Timber
- Human Labor

Ottoman Empire (1299 – 1922 AD)

- Agriculture
- Textiles
- Precious Metals
- Stone
- Spices & Dyes

Mongol Empire (1206 – 1368 AD)

- Land
- Livestock
- Water
- Minerals
- Coal

Spanish Empire (1492 – 1976 AD)

- Gold & Silver
- Agriculture
- Labor
- Livestock
- Shipping Routes

Aztec Empire
(1428 – 1521 AD)

- ► Agricultural
- ► Precious Metals
- ► Cotton and Textiles
- ► Salt and Mineral
  Resources

Inca Empire
(1438 – 1533 AD)

- ► Maize
- ► Textiles
- ► Precious metals
- ► Labor
- ► Water

British Empire
(1603 – 1997 AD)

- ► Sugar
- ► Cotton
- ► Tea
- ► Tobacco & Spices
- ► Gold, Diamonds,
  and Minerals
- ► Coal & Tin

Portuguese Empire
(1415 – 1999 AD)

- ► Spices
- ► Precious Metals
- ► Agriculture
- ► Silk & Textiles
- ► Naval Supremacy
- ► Trade Routes

French Empire
(1534 – 1980 AD)

- ► Grain and Wine
- ► Fur Trade
- ► Coal and Iron Ore
- ► Textiles

Dutch Empire
(1581 – 1975 AD)

- ► Spices
- ► Sugar
- ► Grain
- ► Textiles
- ► Tea & Coffee
- ► Fur & Livestock

The Death of an Empire

What brings down a mighty empire?

It's not simply the passage of time—it's the gradual loss of control over the critical resources that once sustained its power. When an empire's foundation begins to crack and its hold on vital resources weakens, its fall becomes all but inevitable.

So, what led to the collapse of some of history's most powerful empires?

EMPIRE	REASON FOR DOWNFALL	CRITICAL RESOURCE	OUTCOME
Roman Empire	Loss of Grain Supply	Grain from North Africa and Egypt	Rome relied on grain imports to feed its population. As the empire weakened and lost control over these critical regions, food shortages and economic instability contributed to its decline, weakening its ability to maintain its infrastructure and military power.

EMPIRE	REASON FOR DOWNFALL	CRITICAL RESOURCE	OUTCOME
The British Empire	Loss of Colonial Resources	Cotton, tea, rubber, and other raw materials from colonies (e.g., India)	As colonies like India gained independence in the mid-20th century, Britain lost access to vital resources and markets that had fueled its industrial economy. This led to economic decline, reducing Britain's global influence and marking the end of its empire.
The Ottoman Empire	Lost Control over Trade Routes	Key land and sea trade routes between Europe, Asia, and Africa	As European powers found alternative trade routes (like around Africa and through the Suez Canal) and expanded their influence in the Middle East, the Ottoman Empire's economic base weakened. The empire's inability to control critical resources and trade eventually contributed to its collapse after World War I.

EMPIRE	REASON FOR DOWNFALL	CRITICAL RESOURCE	OUTCOME
The Spanish Empire	Loss of Silver from the Americas	Silver from mines in Mexico and Bolivia (Potosí)	Spain's wealth and power in the 16th and 17th centuries were based mainly on silver from the Americas. Over time, inefficiency, inflation, and the depletion of silver mines led to a decline in revenue, contributing to Spain's economic instability and eventual loss of global dominance.
The Soviet Union	Loss of Oil and Gas Reserves	Oil and gas reserves in former Soviet territories (e.g., Azerbaijan, Kazakhstan)	After the collapse of the Soviet Union, Russia lost control of significant oil and gas reserves in newly independent states. This significantly impacted its economy, as these resources were crucial to its global influence and economic stability. While Russia later reasserted dominance in energy markets, the initial loss was destabilizing.

EMPIRE	REASON FOR DOWNFALL	CRITICAL RESOURCE	OUTCOME
The Dutch Empire	Loss of Spice Trade Monopoly	Spices (nutmeg, cloves, pepper) from the East Indies (Indonesia)	The Dutch once dominated the lucrative spice trade in the 17th century. However, competition from the British and declining profits from spices weakened Dutch control. The Dutch empire's economic and political power diminished as they lost their spice monopoly.

When it comes to strategic and critical resources, nations either lead or are led. Control over these resources determines who holds the power and who is subject to it. To secure your future, you must take charge so you're not left at the mercy of others.

Lead or Be Led

Control over critical resources has always placed nations at the top of the global power structure.

Throughout history, the pursuit of resource control and energy dominance has fueled the rise and fall of nations.

There is a clear link between superpower status and self-sufficiency in energy production and consumption.

Countries that rely on others for their resources compromise their power and weaken their political stance. When a nation imports the critical commodities powering its economy and military, it surrenders control to the exporters of those resources.

America's relationship with oil and other countries has limited our foreign policy options. It has also made our economic stability depend on price changes and subject to the political interests of the countries we transact with.

We stand at the beginning of a new era.

As nations compete for control over resources, a new race has emerged: the race towards renewable technologies. This new frontier allows nations to redefine their roles in global politics and trade, reclaim control over supply chains, and reassert influence on the world stage. This shift towards renewable technologies empowers nations to assert their influence more effectively.

Nations that lead in sustainable technology can reduce reliance on adversarial states and strengthen their autonomy.

The next global superpower will be the one that wins the race to renewable technologies. In the quest for supremacy, it's clear: you are either blazing the path or following it.

But there is another significant factor EVERYONE needs to realize...

Our shift away from oil isn't optional—it's essential, as oil is a finite resource!

We must acknowledge this fact before we find ourselves with limited supplies and rising prices, disrupting our economy.

Even more alarming, there's a chance we're already on the backside of oil's lifecycle.

The End of Oil's Economic Life Cycle

The World Energy Outlook 2023, a report from the International Energy Agency (IEA)—a global authority on energy—opens with an alarming statement: "We are on track to see all fossil fuels peak before 2030.'[24]

This isn't just a bold prediction—it's a warning. **Oil is a finite resource**, and oil wells aren't bottomless. Eventually, we'll have no choice but to confront this reality.

As global energy demand continues to grow, driven by population increases and economic development, the pressure on existing oil reserves intensifies.

This leads us to the concept of Peak Oil.

"The term "peak oil" is part of geologist M. King Hubbert's theory developed in 1956 describing the point in time when the maximum rate of global crude oil production is reached, after which crude oil production would enter into terminal decline."[25]

Based on the understanding that oil extraction follows a bell-shaped curve, beyond the peak, production declines and eventually runs out despite increasing demand.

---

24 https://iea.blob.core.windows.net/assets/42b23c45-78bc-4482-b0f9-eb826ae2da3d/World EnergyOutlook2023.pdf

25 https://gardner.utah.edu/peak-oil-theory-revisited/#:~:text=The%20term%20 %E2%80%9Cpeak%20oil%E2%80%9D%20is,would%20enter%20into%20terminal%20decline.

SECRET SILVER
Weather Modification

Silver iodide plays a key role in weather modification through cloud seeding, a process designed to enhance cloud condensation and increase rain or snowfall.

Weather modification efforts have been used in the following locations:

United States: Several western states have cloud seeding programs:

- California
- Colorado
- Idaho
- Nevada
- Utah
- Wyoming

China: Has an extensive weather modification program, particularly for drought mitigation and to ensure clear skies for major events.

United Arab Emirates: Cloud seeding is used to increase rainfall in the desert climate.

Australia: Cloud seeding experiments have been conducted, particularly in Tasmania and parts of mainland Australia.

Thailand: Has used cloud seeding to combat air pollution and drought.

Russia: Has a history of weather modification attempts, including efforts to ensure good weather for public events.

Mexico: Has conducted cloud seeding operations in some areas to combat drought.

Israel: Has a long-standing cloud seeding program to increase rainfall.

Argentina: Has used cloud seeding to mitigate hail damage in agricultural areas.

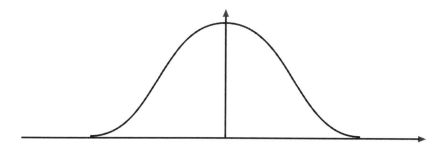

While experts may debate exactly when this peak will occur, the implications are clear: easy-to-access oil is running out. With that comes the potential for severe economic and social upheaval, potentially leading to increased energy prices, shortages, and a pressing need for alternative energy sources.

Let's face it: we are far from the beginning of this curve.

Moving further and further towards — and past the peak — has significant consequences for energy-dependent economies.

Scarcity and rising prices will lead to conflicts over the limited resources remaining.

It's time to accept that we must transition from an oil economy to a new energy economy, a change that protects ourselves and our future.

Whether we like it or not, it's only a matter of time before we exhaust oil reserves and are forced to rely solely on new forms of energy. This reality has accelerated the push towards green technology and renewable energy sources.

The United States has already taken proactive action to start the transition. As a nation, we are moving away from total reliance on fossil fuels and towards renewable energy.

Embracing the transition to renewable energy will give us a leg up on less innovative countries and a head start on establishing global leadership in this emerging energy sector.

However, it's not only for political reasons and because of its limited supply that views on the fossil fuel industry are souring.

There are numerous factors leading society away from oil:

- Climate change - Burning fossil fuels produces green-house gas emissions that cause global warming.
- Air pollution - Extracting, refining, and burning oil creates harmful pollutants.
- Price volatility - Global oil prices swing wildly, causing budget issues.
- Geopolitical risks - Much of the world's oil comes from turbulent regions.

SECRET SILVER
RFID Technology
Radio-Frequency Identification

Silver is essential in constructing Radio-Frequency IDentification tags (AKARFID tags). Each tag is said to contain 10mg of silver! With the demand for this technology skyrocketing, the demand from this one application alone could account for over 10 million ounces of silver.

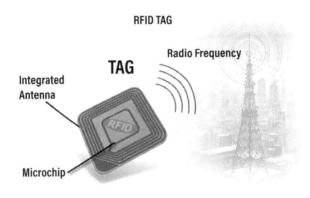

RFID TAG

Radio Frequency

TAG

Integrated Antenna

RFID

Microchip

Use Cases:

Inventory Management in Retail RFID tags attached to products allow retailers to track inventory levels in real-time, reducing stockouts and overstocking. This technology enables faster and more accurate stock counts, improved supply chain visibility, and better theft prevention.

Asset Tracking in Healthcare Hospitals use RFID to track valuable medical equipment, ensuring critical devices can be quickly located when needed. This improves asset utilization, reduces equipment loss, and enhances patient care by minimizing delays in treatment due to missing equipment.

Livestock Management in Agriculture
Farmers use RFID tags to monitor and track individual animals in their herds. This allows for better health monitoring, easier compliance with regulations, and improved traceability in the food supply chain.

Access Control in Security Systems
RFID-enabled key cards or fobs are widely used in office buildings, hotels, and secure facilities to control and monitor access. This technology allows for easy management of access rights and provides a log of entry and exit times for enhanced security.

Supply Chain and Logistics
In logistics and supply chain management, RFID tags on pallets, containers, or individual items enable real-time tracking of goods throughout the shipping process. This improves shipping accuracy, reduces losses, and enhances overall supply chain efficiency.

- Environmental spills - Offshore drilling, fracking, pipelines, and oil transportation have risks of spills and contamination.

As we look out over tomorrow's energy landscape, it's evident that the future demands innovation and a departure from past practices.

The United States, lacking sufficient domestic oil reserves to maintain its superpower status, must lead the transition to renewable energy sources like solar, wind, and hydroelectric power. Despite resistance, this shift is inevitable, and it's better to do it on our terms and seize the opportunities that come with it. In my opinion, the nation that masters renewable technologies first will position itself as the next global superpower. This transition solves our ongoing issues with energy and offers an opportunity for technological leadership on the world stage.

As we transition to renewables, silver will emerge as a cornerstone resource, much like oil once was.

The New Fuel of the Global Economy

The global resource landscape is constantly evolving to meet the world's shifting demands.

Demand has shifted over time from coal to kerosene, then oil, and now renewable energy.

COAL → KEROSENE → OIL → RENEWABLE ENERGY

Oil has shaped significant events over the past century, but its era is ending as silver rises to power the next generation of critical technologies.

Silver is set to become indispensable in this new energy era, powering the critical technologies and infrastructure that will define a sustainable future.

We must build the infrastructure to accelerate our transition to renewable energy.

This isn't something that can happen overnight, so we need to start now.

For decades, leaders have called for energy independence—now is the time to make it a reality.

To maintain our leadership on the global stage, we must diversify our energy sources, increase our use of alternative energy sources, and push the country toward a more sustainable and resilient future.

With this shift, we solidify our place at the top and boost our economy by creating new areas of growth and advancement.

So, what does our future look like when powered by renewable energy?

2022 Electricity Generation Facts

- 4,231 billion kilowatt hours of electricity were generated.
- 60% was from fossil fuels—coal, natural gas, petroleum, and other gases
- 21% was from renewable energy sources
- 18% was from nuclear energy
- An additional 61 billion kWh of electricity generation was from small-scale solar photovoltaic systems.[26]

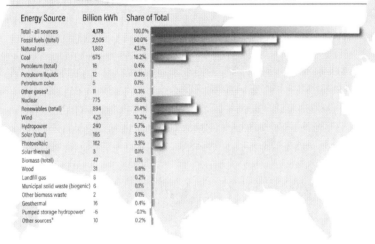

U.S. ELECTRICITY GENERATION BY ENERGY SOURCE

Energy Source	Billion kWh	Share of Total
Total - all sources	4,178	100.0%
Fossil fuels (total)	2,505	60.0%
Natural gas	1,802	43.1%
Coal	675	16.2%
Petroleum (total)	16	0.4%
Petroleum liquids	12	0.3%
Petroleum coke	5	0.1%
Other gases³	11	0.3%
Nuclear	775	18.6%
Renewables (total)	894	21.4%
Wind	425	10.2%
Hydropower	240	5.7%
Solar (total)	165	3.9%
Photovoltaic	162	3.9%
Solar thermal	3	0.1%
Biomass (total)	47	1.1%
Wood	31	0.8%
Landfill gas	8	0.2%
Municipal solid waste (biogenic)	6	0.1%
Other biomass waste	2	0.1%
Geothermal	16	0.4%
Pumped storage hydropower⁴	-6	-0.1%
Other sources⁵	10	0.2%

---

26 https://www.eia.gov/tools/faqs/faq.php?id=427&t=6

Replacing Oil With Renewable Energy

While the 20th century ran on oil, the 21st will run on renewables.

What would it take to replace oil with green technology?

"In 2022, the United States consumed an average of about 20.01 million barrels of petroleum per day."[27]

To break that down, the "U.S. crude oil production equaled about 11.911 million barrels per day, crude oil imports equaled about 6.281 million barrels per day, and crude oil exports equaled about 3.576 million barrels per day."[28]

These production and import figures show how central oil is to our economy. The budgetary considerations alone are mind-blowing. Between 2020 and 2024, Congress issued over $5.7 billion in tax relief to the oil and gas industries.[29]

Moving away from this dependence will require addressing the significant economic gap and meeting our energy needs through alternative and renewable sources.

The good news is we're already making progress in closing this gap.

---

27 https://www.eia.gov/tools/faqs/faq.php?id=33&t=6
28 https://www.eia.gov/tools/faqs/faq.php?id=33&t=6
29 https://css.umich.edu/publications/factsheets/energy/us-renewable-energy-factsheet

The U.S. Energy Information Administration's (EIA) 2023 report on electricity generation reveals promising developments:

"We expect that the 23 gigawatts (GW) in 2023 and 37 GW in 2024 of new solar capacity scheduled to come online will help U.S. solar generation grow by 15% in 2023 and 39% in 2024. We expect solar and wind generation together in 2024 to overtake electric power generation from coal for the first year ever, exceeding coal by nearly 90 billion kilowatt hours."[30]

> **SECRET SILVER**
> **Pottery Glaze**
> Silver, in the form of silver chloride, has unique properties and can be used in pottery to give it an exquisite glaze luster.

This milestone—solar and wind surpassing coal for the first time—is a powerful step toward energy independence.

Transitioning to a sustainable future demands policies that encourage innovation, support clean energy technologies, and enable a gradual reduction of our oil dependence.[31]

TIMELINE FOR CHANGES IN THE GLOBAL ENERGY SYSTEM

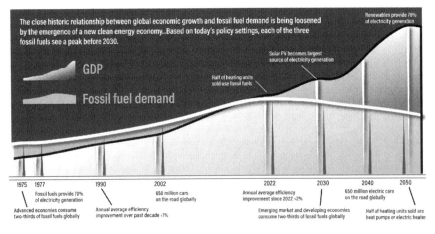

---

30 https://www.eia.gov/outlooks/steo/
31 https://www.iea.org/reports/world-energy-outlook-2023/pathways-for-the-energy-mix

The Biden administration has made strides in setting such policies, creating a more straightforward path forward for the clean energy transition.

While I support the transition to renewable energy, I disagree with aspects of Biden's green energy bill and the Inflation Reduction Act.

Some provisions are overly progressive and exceed what's necessary. My main concern is the heavy reliance on taxpayer-funded incentives and subsidies.

We can achieve our energy goals through a more balanced approach that encourages innovation without excessive government intervention and handouts.

"In signing the Inflation Reduction Act last year, the President also secured the largest investment to advance energy security and combat climate change in American history."[32]

"The President's Budget invests a total of $52.2 billion in discretionary budget authority to tackle the climate crisis, $10.9 billion more than FY 2023 or an increase of nearly 26 percent"[33]

Biden's plan also calls to reduce "fossil fuel subsidies, replacing the subsidies with incentives to start producing green energy."[34]

"Biden has ordered the amount of energy produced from offshore wind turbines to be doubled by 2030."[35]

The shift toward green energy is accelerating both production and demand for sustainable technologies, driving up the consumption of essential resources needed to power them.

---

32 https://www.whitehouse.gov/omb/briefing-room/2023/03/09/fact-sheet-president-bidens-budget-lowers-energy-costs-combats-the-climate-crisis-and-advances-environmental-justice/

33 https://www.whitehouse.gov/omb/briefing-room/2023/03/09/fact-sheet-president-bidens-budget-lowers-energy-costs-combats-the-climate-crisis-and-advances-environmental-justice/

34 https://en.wikipedia.org/wiki/Environmental_policy_of_the_Joe_Biden_administration#Energy_efficiency

35 https://en.wikipedia.org/wiki/Environmental_policy_of_the_Joe_Biden_administration#Energy_efficiency

And as this transformation gains momentum, one resource will be at the heart of it all:

Silver.

Silver is the Linchpin of the Renewable Energy Revolution

The Cambridge Dictionary defines "linchpin" as:

"The most important member of a group or part of a system, that holds together the other members or parts or makes it possible for them to operate as intended." [36]

For the new energy economy, silver is that linchpin.

The future of clean energy hinges on a steady supply of silver, as its unique properties align perfectly with the needs of the 21st century:

SECRET SILVER
Edible Silver
In South Asian cuisine, edible silver foil is used to garnish sweets and delicacies. While the foil has no flavor, it makes dishes visually stunning.

- **Highest Electrical and Thermal Conductivity:** Enables efficient energy transmission, essential for batteries, circuits, and solar technologies.

---

36   https://dictionary.cambridge.org/us/dictionary/english/linchpin

- **Ductility and Flexibility:** Silver can be drawn into thin, flexible wires, which are ideal for electronic components and advanced battery designs.
- **High Reflectivity:** Silver's high reflectivity is invaluable in solar mirrors and optical instruments, maximizing light capture and energy efficiency.
- **Antimicrobial Qualities:** Its natural oligodynamic effect inhibits bacterial growth, enhancing applications in medical technology and clean water systems.
- **Photosensitivity:** Silver nitrate reacts to light, making it crucial for solar panel and imaging technologies.
- **Recyclability:** Silver can be reused without losing its properties, supporting a sustainable supply chain.
- **Precious:** Silver's relative scarcity and intrinsic value make it highly prized across cultures and industries.
- **Dense and Workable:** Dense yet malleable, silver is easy to mint and shape, from industrial components to fine jewelry.
- **Inertness:** High resistance to corrosion ensures durability in demanding industrial and environmental conditions.

Silver's unmatched versatility and critical role in sustainable energy applications make it a key investment for the future. As renewable technologies expand, silver remains indispensable, supporting the transition to a resilient and eco-friendly energy economy.

EVs Drive Silver Demand

"From 2021 to 2022, the number of electric cars sold almost doubled, breaking records and increasing from 3.75 million to 6.75 million globally.

In 2021, more electric vehicles were sold in a single week than during all of 2012.

Electric cars depend heavily on silver. Each EV contains between 25 and 50 grams of silver, depending on the model, and hybrid vehicles use 18 to 34 grams of silver.

Silver's electrical and thermal conductivity makes it an ideal material for automobile batteries. It is also ideal for use in EVs because it is non-toxic and hypoallergenic.

Overall, the automotive sector uses 55 million ounces of silver annually, and by 2025, that amount is anticipated to increase to 90 million ounces. The demand for silver in the automotive industry, and for the creation of renewable energy, will only increase, which will inevitably drive the silver market's growth."[37]

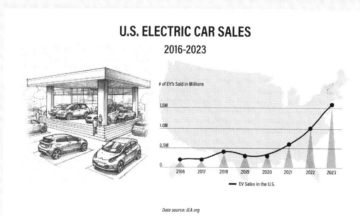

U.S. ELECTRIC CAR SALES
2016-2023

# of EV's Sold in Millions

— EV Sales in the U.S.

Data source: IEA.org

---

37   https://newsdirect.com/news/ev-demand-could-have-a-major-effect-on-the-price-of-silver-590610436

Green Technology
Facts & Figures

The demand for clean, sustainable energy sources is a critical driver in today's energy portfolio. At the center of the shift towards renewable energy is silver, a resource reshaping how we harness and consume power.

Silver is indispensable in nearly every type of green technology currently in use or development.

Solar

Silver plays a fundamental role in solar energy production.

Photovoltaic Demand — "Use in photovoltaics - solar panels - increased to 140.3 million ounces of silver in 2022."[38] Resulting in "a record 220 gigawatts (GW) of solar capacity... added in 2022."[39]

How exactly is silver used in solar panels?

"When manufacturers produce panels, they prepare a silver paste, then use the screen printing process and high

---

38   https://www.silverinstitute.org/silver-solar-technology-2/
39   https://www.iea.org/reports/world-energy-outlook-2023/pathways-for-the-energy-mix

temperatures to make the thin silver lines that can be seen on the outside of the panels' photovoltaic cells."[40]

"An average solar panel of two square meters in size uses about 20 grams of silver, so the photovoltaic industry consumes about 8% of the world's silver supply annually."[41]

The facility will produce 6.09 billion kilowatt hours of electricity annually, sufficient to meet the energy needs of Papua New Guinea or Luxembourg for one year.

DID YOU KNOW:
The world's largest solar farm is the Xinjiang solar farm in China, which spans 200,000 acres and has an installed solar capacity of 5 gigawatts.[42]

Look at that number again — solar power uses 8% of the world's supply of silver!

The growing acceptance and expansion of solar technology highlight the long-term resource demands for silver.

---

40 https://news.virginia.edu/content/uva-effort-mine-silver-old-solar-panels-receives-250k-doe-support

41 https://news.virginia.edu/content/uva-effort-mine-silver-old-solar-panels-receives-250k-doe-support

42 https://www.power-technology.com/news/china-5gw-solar-farm-xinjiang/

SOLAR PANEL FABRICATION CREATES RECORD SILVER DEMAND

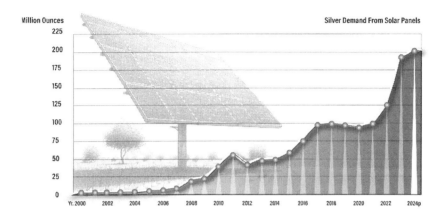

And Demand Is Increasing

Solar energy technology is expanding rapidly as it gains global popularity and acceptance.

The EIA—the U.S. Department of Energy Information Administration—"predicts a 38% increase in solar electricity generation in 2024 from its 2023 level."[43]

The impact of this growth is twofold:

1. **Rising Demand:** The production and maintenance of solar panels will consume silver supplies, creating ongoing pressure on global reserves.

2. **Limited Panel Lifespan:** "Solar panels have a useful life of up to 25 years. Manufacturers don't tend to refurbish the panels after that because of costs."[44] This means

---

43 https://pv-magazine-usa.com/2023/12/18/38-solar-growth-pushing-wind-solar-dynamic-duo-past-coal-in-2024/#:~:text=The%20EIA%20predicts%20a%2038,projected%20at%20599%20billion%20kWh.

44 https://news.virginia.edu/content/uva-effort-mine-silver-old-solar-panels-receives-250k-doe-support

a full-scale transition to solar energy isn't a one-time investment; it requires sustained resources and production for replacement and expansion.

If we are going to make a complete transition to solar, we must recognize that this shift requires ongoing resources and infrastructure development. Solar energy isn't a one-time setup—it demands a steady supply of silver to create, maintain, and eventually replace solar panels over time.

The move toward a sustainable future calls for strategic investment in these resources now to make sure we have the capacity to support solar power at scale for generations to come.

Demand for silver for photovoltaics worldwide from 2014 to 2022, with a forecast for 2023 (in million ounces)

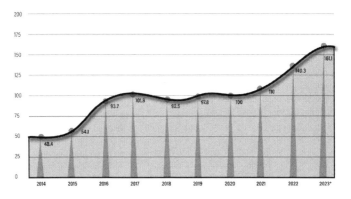

Electric Vehicles

As the automotive industry shifts toward electric power, silver has become an indispensable resource. "Each EV contains between 25 and 50 grams of silver, depending on the model, and hybrid cars use 18 to 34 grams of silver."[45]

---

45 https://finance.yahoo.com/news/ev-demand-could-major-effect-140000881.html#:~: text=Electric%20cars%20depend%20heavily%20on,to%2034%20grams%20of%20silver.

The sector is expanding rapidly. According to Yahoo Finance, "In 2021, more electric vehicles were sold in one week than in the whole of 2012." [46] This explosive growth is placing unprecedented pressure on the global silver supply.

Demand for EVs is only expected to increase. The Silver Institute projects that "the move to autonomous driving should lead to a dramatic escalation of vehicle complexity, requiring even more silver consumption."[47] The Silver Institute released a report with "projections of nearly 90 million ounces (Moz) of silver absorbed annually in the automotive industry by 2025." [48]

With the demand for EVs surging, silver is poised to play an essential role in powering the automotive future and meeting the needs of a rapidly evolving market.

Share of New Cars sold that are Electric, 2023
Electric cars include fully battery-electric and plug-in-hybrids.

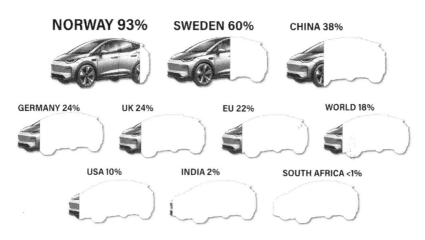

NORWAY 93%   SWEDEN 60%   CHINA 38%

GERMANY 24%   UK 24%   EU 22%   WORLD 18%

USA 10%   INDIA 2%   SOUTH AFRICA <1%

46 https://finance.yahoo.com/news/ev-demand-could-major-effect-140000881.html#:~:
    text=Electric%20cars%20depend%20heavily%20on,to%2034%20grams%20of%20silver.
47 https://kinesis.money/blog/silver/evs-reshaping-silver-market-investment/
48 https://www.silverinstitute.org/silver-consumption-global-automotive-sector-approach-
    90-million-ounces-2025/

The Dual-Vehicle Future

As an investor and automotive enthusiast, I've closely followed the shifts in vehicle ownership. Rising oil costs and advancements in electric vehicle (EV) technology are leading us toward a "Dual-Vehicle Future."

When examining inflation, wage growth, and the rising costs of traditional vehicle ownership, a clear trend emerges: the general public may soon view gas-powered cars as a luxury, increasingly turning to alternatives like ridesharing, public transit, or more economical options. This is where electric vehicles are set to fill the gap left by increasingly costly combustion-engine cars.

Enter the everyday EV

As EV technology progresses, I envision a future where many households own an EV for daily commutes and around-town driving and, if affordable, keep a gas-powered car for longer trips.

This dual-vehicle scenario combines the economic and environmental benefits of EVs for daily use with the long-range reliability and driving enjoyment of gas vehicles for occasional longer journeys.

Economy of EVs

From an investment perspective, the financial benefits of EVs are as compelling as their environmental impact. These advantages will likely drive widespread EV adoption, sustaining demand for silver and other critical materials essential to this market shift.

2024 Tesla Model 3 Long Range AWD-E	2024 Ford F150 Pickup 4WD	2024 Toyota Sienna 2WD	2024 BMW 530i Sedan
◀ Electric Vehicle	⛽ Gasoline Vehicle	⛽ Hybrid Vehicle Gasoline	⛽ Hybrid Vehicle Gasoline
Total Range 341 m	Total Range 720 m	Total Range 648 m	Total Range 477 m

Annual Fuel Cost $1,000	$3,400	$1,900	$2,250
Cost to Drive 25 Miles $1.65	$5.62	$3.12	$3.75
Cost to Fill the Tank $20.50	$162	$81	$72
Tank Size 82 kWh	36 gallons	18 gallons	15.9 gallons

The most immediate economic benefit of EVs is their lower fuel costs. Electricity is generally cheaper than gasoline, resulting in significantly lower per-mile costs for EV owners. Over a vehicle's lifetime, these savings provide a strong economic incentive for consumers.

VEHICLE	FUEL	COST	MPG/kWh[49]	COST PER MILE
CAR	ELECTRIC	$0.23/kWh	3 miles per kWh	$0.076 / mile
CAR	GAS	$4.50/gallon	33 miles per gallon	$0.136 / mile
TRUCK	GAS	$4.50/gallon	23 miles per gallon	$0.195 / mile

Based on fuel costs alone, driving a gas car is 55% more expensive, and driving a gas truck is 256% more expensive than an electric vehicle.

But that's only accounting for fuel. EVs also offer reduced maintenance costs due to their simpler mechanical structure:

---

49   https://www.energy.gov/eere/vehicles/articles/fotw-1306-september-4-2023-model-year-2022-light-duty-vehicles-sold-us#:~:text=Vehicle%20Technologies%20Office-,FOTW%20%231306%2C%20September%204%2C%202023:%20Model%20Year%202022,Averaged%2026.4%20Miles%20Per%20Gallon&text=The%20production%2Dweighted%20average%20fuel,Automotive%20Trends%20Report%20%2C%20December%202022.

- No oil changes are required
- Reduced brake wear thanks to regenerative braking
- Fewer fluids to replace
- No spark plugs or timing belts to change

Over time, these reduced maintenance needs translate to substantial savings, further enhancing the economic appeal of EVs.

When considering the total cost of ownership—factoring in fuel savings, lower maintenance costs, and potential tax incentives—EVs often prove more economical than comparable gas-powered vehicles, even with a higher initial purchase price.

This long-term economic advantage will be a key driver in their adoption as Americans start to look for ways to stretch their dollars and maintain their lifestyles.

While I cherish my gas-powered cars, I recognize that the future of everyday transportation is electric. The dual-vehicle future—with EVs for daily use and gas vehicles for longer trips and enjoyment—presents a practical transition that balances economic realities with driving pleasure.

This shift is part of the growing opportunity in the silver market.

But it's more than just the cars themselves.

The entire EV infrastructure requires even MORE silver to power charging stations.

It's almost hard to think of something within the EV ecosystem that doesn't utilize silver. Silver is in every aspect of a modern electric vehicle: electronics, wiring, powertrains, and charging.

Selected Automotive Electrical & Electronic Components

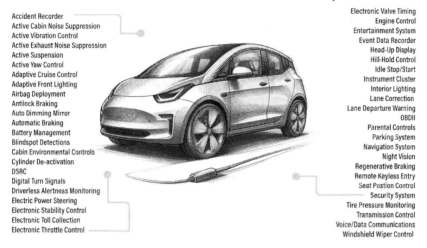

Accident Recorder
Active Cabin Noise Suppression
Active Vibration Control
Active Exhaust Noise Suppression
Active Suspension
Active Yaw Control
Adaptive Cruise Control
Adaptive Front Lighting
Airbag Deployment
Antilock Braking
Auto Dimming Mirror
Automatic Braking
Battery Management
Blindspot Detections
Cabin Environmental Controls
Cylinder De-activation
DSRC
Digital Turn Signals
Driverless Alertness Monitoring
Electric Power Steering
Electronic Stability Control
Electronic Toll Collection
Electronic Throttle Control

Electronic Valve Timing
Engine Control
Entertainment System
Event Data Recorder
Head-Up Display
Hill-Hold Control
Idle Stop/Start
Instrument Cluster
Interior Lighting
Lane Correction
Lane Departure Warning
OBDII
Parental Controls
Parking System
Navigation System
Night Vision
Regenerative Braking
Remote Keyless Entry
Seat Postion Control
Security System
Tire Pressure Monitoring
Transmission Control
Voice/Data Communications
Windshield Wiper Control

And there's one area that is evolving and will further drain the silver supply:

Battery Packs[50]

Samsung recently unveiled a groundbreaking silver solid-state battery, a technological leap that could reshape the landscape of electric vehicles and the precious metals market.

This innovation addresses some of the most pressing challenges facing the EV industry and could drive a significant surge in silver demand.

Samsung reportedly achieved a breakthrough in solid-state battery technology, successfully incorporating silver-carbon composite anodes into high-performance, all-solid-state batteries for electric vehicles.

---

50 https://talkmarkets.com/content/news/silver-demand-to-soar-with-breakthrough-of-samsung-silver-solid-state-battery?post=459058

This innovation promises to deliver significant improvements in battery technology, and the resulting benefits are like a dream come true for EV enthusiasts.

Unprecedented Range: With a single charge capable of powering an EV for up to 600 miles, range anxiety could become a thing of the past. This extended range rivals and even surpasses that of many conventional gas-powered vehicles, marking a significant milestone in EV adoption.

Longevity: The new batteries boast a projected lifespan of 20 years, potentially outlasting the vehicles they power. This longevity reduces the environmental impact of battery production and promises to dramatically lower the total cost of EV ownership.

Lightning-Fast Charging: The most impressive feature is the battery's ability to fully charge in just nine minutes. This rapid charging capability eliminates one of the major inconveniences of EV ownership, making long-distance travel more feasible and convenient.

Compact: With an energy density of 500 Wh/kg, these batteries pack nearly twice the power of current mainstream EV batteries into the same space. This increased density allows for smaller, lighter batteries or a significantly extended range without adding bulk.

Safety: By utilizing a solid electrolyte instead of a liquid one, Samsung has markedly reduced the risk of battery fires—a concern that has plagued the EV industry. This enhancement in safety could boost consumer confidence and accelerate EV adoption rates.

While Samsung's breakthrough is exciting, it's important to note that the journey from laboratory to mass production can be long and full of challenges. However, if successfully brought to market, these silver solid-state batteries could start a new era in EV technology and have implications beyond the automotive sector.

The use of silver in these cutting-edge batteries could have profound implications for the precious metals market. This increased demand will come at a time when silver is already seeing growing industrial use in solar panels and electronics, which could drain the supply and squeeze silver prices.

Breakthroughs like this underscore the critical role that silver will play in shaping our energy future.

Beyond batteries, silver's role in sustainable energy extends even further, playing a crucial part in various power generation methods like:

Wind Turbines

Wind turbines are critical to expanding our renewable energy infrastructure, and silver is increasingly important in making them more durable. One essential component of wind turbines is the brush—an electrical conductor that enables efficient energy transfer. Wind farm operators are turning to silver brushes as a "wiser choice for longevity and lifetime performance"[51] due to silver's unique anti-corrosive properties. Resistant to harsh environmental conditions, silver brushes help ensure reliable, long-lasting operation, even in the harshest climates.

Energy Storage

Capturing excess energy requires reliable storage systems to prevent waste. As demand for on-demand energy storage grows,

---

51   https://www.windpowerengineering.com/copper-or-silver-how-to-choose-reliable-wind-turbine-brushes/#google_vignette

batteries will become an increasingly critical segment of green technology—and silver will be at the core of this transformation.

Silver's conductivity boosts battery efficiency and longevity, making it indispensable in energy storage systems that power everything from handheld devices to the electric grid. Beyond green tech, silver will also fuel a range of groundbreaking innovations, ensuring reliable, high-performance systems in future technology.

As we move towards a future where energy needs are constantly evolving, silver will continue to be the foundation for advancing sustainable, efficient energy solutions.

Silver fuels the groundbreaking technologies that will define our future.

PART 4
Silver's Saturation Point

Silver in Your Daily Life

I see striking similarities when I look at the future of silver compared to oil.

Both commodities impact our daily lives far more than we often realize.

Consider all the ways we encounter oil every day.

Like oil, silver will soon become just as ubiquitous.

If something has a switch, screen, or circuit, it contains silver.

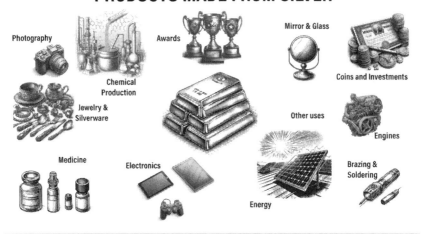

PRODUCTS MADE FROM SILVER

Photography
Awards
Mirror & Glass
Coins and Investments
Chemical Production
Jewelry & Silverware
Other uses
Engines
Medicine
Electronics
Brazing & Soldering
Energy

Silver's unique properties are the foundation of modern technology, powering countless devices we rely on every day. How many of these do you use daily?

- Computer
- Smartphone
- Tablet
- Television
- Electronic gadgets
- Wearable electronics
- Kitchen Appliances
- Speakers
- Radios
- Car

SECRET SILVER
Deodorant
Stay fresh all day with deodorants enhanced with silver chloride. Silver is known for its odor-fighting properties, keeping you confident and odor-free.

Silver's essential role extends far beyond electronics. It's used in countless smaller, often-overlooked applications across various industries, creating a significant, steady daily demand.

This 'long-tail' demand emphasizes how indispensable silver has become to modern life.

Healthcare

Silver's antimicrobial properties make it indispensable in healthcare, where it plays a role in nearly every area:

- Medical equipment
- Silver-coated instruments
- Wound dressings
- Catheters
- Implants
- Sensors
- Surgical instruments
- Nanoparticles - "Silver nanoparticles are widely used, with over 500 tons of annual global production and a market size of over $2 billion per year."[52]

As the U.S. population ages, demand for medical products and devices will continue to rise. The needs of an aging population, especially the baby boomer generation, will drive sustained growth in the medical industry, increasing demand for silver in healthcare applications.

Silver In Clothing

Silver's natural antimicrobial properties help clothing combat odors and keep fabrics fresh. Silver-infused garments resist odors, kill bacteria, and inhibit fungal growth, making them ideal for activewear and everyday use.

---

52   https://news.virginia.edu/content/uva-effort-mine-silver-old-solar-panels-receives-250k-doe-support

Purification & Filtration

Silver nanoparticles are invaluable in removing environmental toxins through water purification and air filtration systems. As society pushes to reduce the number of viruses and microorganisms in our surroundings, silver plays a crucial role in disinfecting and neutralizing harmful contaminants in both air and water, meeting the growing demand for safer, cleaner environments.

SECRET SILVER
Biowear
Ralph Lauren revolutionized fashion and technology at the 2014 US Open when it debuted their cutting-edge shirt embedded with bio-sensing silver fibers. This high-tech garment utilizes sensors that can communicate directly with your smartphone via Bluetooth, providing real-time insights into your heart rate, stress levels, and breathing rates.

Real-World Examples

Silver's application in water purification is revolutionizing access to clean water in developing and low-resource regions. This precious metal makes a life-changing difference in communities that have long struggled with waterborne diseases and limited access to safe drinking water.

Rural India: Silver-infused ceramic filters provide families access to clean drinking water and reduce waterborne diseases. The Tata Swach filter, developed by Tata Chemicals, uses rice husk ash impregnated with silver nanoparticles to remove 99% of surface water contaminants.

Sub-Saharan Africa: NGOs (Non-governmental organizations) distribute silver-based water purification tablets, offering a simple yet effective solution for communities lacking central-ized water treatment facilities.

Urban Bangladesh: Stanford University and BRAC have collaborated to introduce silver-coated ceramic tablets for household water treatment in Dhaka's slums. These tablets have significantly reduced E. coli contamination, improving water quality for thousands of families.

Disaster Relief in Haiti: Following the 2010 earthquake, silver-based water purification systems were crucial in providing safe drinking water to displaced communities. Organizations like Potters for Peace distributed silver-infused ceramic filters, helping to prevent the spread of waterborne diseases in emergency shelters.

Remote Communities in Mexico: The Cántaro Azul Foundation has implemented a UV-based water disinfection system that uses silver ions to maintain water purity during storage. This technology has brought clean water to over 25,000 people in rural Mexico.

Refugee Camps in Jordan: UNHCR has piloted silver-based water purification systems in Za'atari refugee camp, one of the largest Syrian refugee camps. These systems have helped ensure a steady, clean water supply in challenging conditions.

Schools in Kenya: The Silver Nano-Enabled Water Treatment Technology project, supported by USAID, has installed silver nanoparticle-based water filters in rural Kenya, improving student health and attendance.

Municipalities in China: Several cities in China are experimenting with large-scale water treatment plants that incorporate silver nanoparticle technology. These plants aim to address microbial contamination and chemical pollutants in urban water supplies.

Household Applications in Brazil: Local initiatives in Brazil's favelas have introduced affordable, silver-infused water bottles and jerry cans. These containers help maintain water purity during collection and storage, a critical issue in areas with intermittent water supply.

Silver's Role in Environmental Purification

Beyond water purification, silver plays an essential role in air filtration, meeting society's growing need to reduce exposure to harmful microorganisms and toxins:

- Silver-infused air filters in hospitals and public spaces reduce the spread of airborne pathogens.
- Silver-based air purifiers enhance indoor air quality by neutralizing pollutants and allergens in homes and offices.

Silver's role in creating a cleaner, safer world will only expand as awareness of global health and environmental challenges grows.

Industrial Applications

While modern innovations continue to find new uses for silver, many of its traditional applications remain central to **foundational industries**. A few of these legacy uses include:

- Steel Ball Bearings
  - "Not only is a silver-coated steel ball bearing strong, but the silver acts as a lubricant, reducing friction between the bearing and its housing. This increases the performance and longevity of the engine."[53]

---

53 https://www.silverinstitute.org/silver-bearings/

- Mirrors
- Optical instruments
- Telescopes
- Microscopes
- Electroplating
- Brazing & Soldering — joining pipes and wire
- Traditional Photography - although not used much today.
- Silverware
- Jewelry

Beyond these uses, the military and defense industry remains one of the largest drivers of silver demand. Silver's unique properties make it indispensable in military applications, where durability, conductivity, and reliability are non-negotiable. Let's explore how silver powers critical defense technologies and supports national security.

Wartime Silver

One of the most controversial uses of silver is its role in manufacturing advanced weaponry, sparking both ethical and practical discussions around its demand.

While this topic is polarizing and involves significant ethical and moral considerations, we have to discuss it as it remains a constant source of demand for the precious metal.

Top Secret Silver

The exact details and amounts of silver used in military applications are highly classified.

As I explored this topic, I saw drastically different opinions on the quantity of silver our defense department uses.

For example, one source claims a Tomahawk missile contains between 10 and 15 ounces of silver, and another argues it contains over 500 ounces. That is such a wide gap, and the truth is, there is no way a civilian could know the exact amount of silver used in the production of military equipment. Our government would never jeopardize national security by releasing these details.

This section does not provide specific information but highlights that silver is crucial for military operations. It doesn't take security clearance to know that silver's electrical and thermal conductivity and durability make it a necessary component in the defense sector.

While I don't know the exact details, I am confident that silver is intertwined with our nation's safety. It's not just the United States. Countries around the globe worldwide rely on silver for the proper functioning of their weapon defense systems.

Even more important, the silver used in warfare is often single-use, particularly in munitions and missile systems. Once deployed, the silver and other materials are lost forever, contributing to ongoing resource depletion and driving up demand for fresh metal supplies.

Here is how militaries around the globe utilize silver:

- Missiles
- Fighter jets
- Satellites
- Tanks
- Submarines
- Torpedoes
- Night vision goggles
- Communication devices
- Radar
- Nuclear technology

Given the emphasis on precision and reliability in modern military technology, it's no surprise that it relies heavily on electronic components—making silver an essential element fueling modern warfare.

Let's explore a few of the more intriguing uses.

Missile Technology

Missiles are some of the most advanced weapons in the military arsenal, and their critical components rely on silver to function effectively.

Guidance Systems

These systems utilize intricate networks of sensors, circuits, and switches, all of which require reliable electrical connections. Silver ensures rapid and precise signal transmission.

DID YOU KNOW:
The United States spent approximately $916 billion on military defense in 2023, which is larger than the next nine countries' military spending combined (China, Russia, India, Saudi Arabia, United Kingdom, Germany, Ukraine, France, and Japan)[54]

---

54   https://www.pgpf.org/infographic/infographic-the-facts-about-us-defense-spending

Propulsion Systems

Silver coatings help manage the extreme heat generated during launch and flight.

Detonation Mechanisms

The dependable conductivity of silver ensures detonation signals are transmitted even under the harshest conditions.

Control Systems

Smart bombs employ adjustable fins and other control mechanisms that guide the bomb to its target after release. Silver provides responsive and reliable operation.

Communications Equipment

In military operations, where communication is vital, silver is indispensable in producing high-frequency radio devices and secure communication setups. Silver-based components are essential for these systems, ensuring enhanced signal transmission with minimal loss—a critical advantage in battlefield scenarios.

Satellites Equipment

Satellites operate in an unforgiving space environment. Silver's reflective properties and resistance to extreme conditions make it ideal for components that must perform reliably in such a harsh atmosphere.

Radar

Silver-coated components are essential in detecting enemy aircraft and ships.

Surveillance and Reconnaissance

Silver is essential in producing high-definition imaging systems, including thermal and infrared cameras.

Nuclear Technology

Silver's unique properties make it indispensable in nuclear applications, especially within the reactors powering submarines and aircraft carriers. Its high thermal and electrical conductivity are crucial in managing the intense heat produced during nuclear reactions. But silver's true value lies in a property that sets it apart in nuclear technology: its ability to absorb neutrons effectively. This function is essential for reactor safety, as neutron absorption plays a critical role in controlling nuclear reactions and maintaining stable power output.

In neutron absorption, silver combines with indium and cadmium in reactor control rods. These rods regulate the fission rate within the reactor core, preventing overheating and ensuring a controlled release of energy. This role is critical in maintaining efficiency and safety standards, particularly in high-stakes environments like nuclear-powered vessels.

Silver also contributes to heat exchange systems within nuclear reactors. As a cooling system component, silver assists in dissipating heat, further safeguarding reactor stability during operation.

A Pillar of National Security Technology

Silver's significance in modern warfare and defense is undeniable. From stealth technology to cutting-edge electrical systems, the demand for sophisticated, reliable, and efficient systems will only increase—solidifying silver's essential role.

As military technology races forward, silver's role is set to skyrocket. From radar-evading aircraft skin to lightning-fast battlefield communications, silver is delivering victory through innovation. In the high-stakes game of global security, silver is mission-critical.

THE SILVER LINING OF THE MOBILE PHONE MARKET

You have more silver around you than you realize.

Scientists at The University of Plymouth found that each mobile phone contains roughly 90mg of silver.[55] When you factor in that 1.5 billion smartphones are produced each year, that comes to almost 4.3 million oz of silver.[56]

A staggering fact is that 7275 Metric Tons of silver are consumed annually for the manufacturing of mobile phones, laptops, and other electronic equipment.

Not recycling this silver depletes our natural resources and contributes to environmental pollution.

Furthermore, for every 1 million cell phones that are recycled, 35,274 lbs of copper, 772 lbs of silver, 75 lbs of gold, and 33 lbs of palladium can be recovered.[57]

---

55 https://www.metaltechnews.com/story/2020/01/01/tech-metals/miracle-of-metals-make-smartphones-smart/114.html#:~:text=The%20University%20of%20Plymouth%20scientists,billion%20smartphones%20produced%20each%20year.
56 Thomson Reuters GFMS, 2014
57 https://www.dosomething.org/us/facts/11-facts-about-e-waste#fnref7

For every 1 million cell phones that are recycled, 35,274 lbs of copper, 772 lbs of silver, 75 lbs of gold, and 33 lbs of palladium can be recovered.

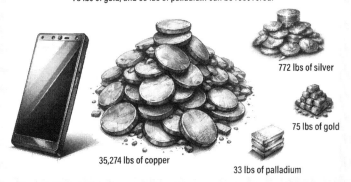

772 lbs of silver

75 lbs of gold

35,274 lbs of copper

33 lbs of palladium

But the sad fact is that only 12.5% of e-waste is currently recycled.[58]

Only 12.5% of e-waste is currently recycled

Most of the metals used to make electronics are lost to landfills.

Let's change this trend by recycling our e-waste and saving these precious metals from being wasted.

---

58   https://www.dosomething.org/us/facts/11-facts-about-e-waste#fnref7

Silver Is at the Forefront of Innovation

Silver is a critical component in groundbreaking technologies that are reshaping our world.

From powering the intricate networks of crypto mining and 5G to enabling immersive virtual and augmented reality experiences, silver is connecting our present to an electrifying future.

Let's explore these emerging industries, discover how silver is utilized, and learn how its role in these cutting-edge technologies drives demand for this limited resource.

Quantum Computing

I'll admit that this was an entirely new technology to me, but my research has shown that while it is new, it is growing rapidly.

This section might be optional for those already well-versed in qubits and cryogenic environments. But if you're like me and thought a qubit was the latest Pokémon character, pay attention.

What is qubit, and how does it relate to the latest computer technology?

We all know that standard computers, like laptops and desktops, operate using bits. A bit is the smallest unit of data, representing either a 0 or a 1—meaning it can be either off (0) or on (1).

A quantum bit—A.K.A. qubit—can, thanks to the principles of quantum mechanics, simultaneously be both 0 and 1, meaning it can be both on and off simultaneously.

While the underlying science is complex and beyond the scope of this book, this unique capability of qubits is fundamentally changing the nature of computing and propelling us into a new technological frontier.

Currently, quantum computing is far from mainstream and is only being utilized by the most well-funded industries.

- **Pharmaceuticals and Healthcare**
- **Finance**
- **Cybersecurity**
- **Transportation**
- **Energy Sector**
- **Automotive and Manufacturing**
- **Telecommunications**

How does silver factor into this new technology?

Qubits

Superconducting qubits operate at extremely low temperatures and require materials with excellent conductive properties to minimize energy losses. Using silver in the design of these qubits will improve performance and reduce losses due to electrical resistance.

Cryogenic Environments

Qubits are incredibly delicate and must be kept at freezing temperatures, isolated from environmental disturbances. Silver is used to construct cylindrical containers that house them and help maintain super-low temperatures, ensuring the quantum system remains stable for as long as needed.

Connectivity and Readouts

Silver is used in the wiring and connectors within quantum computers to ensure that interactions with qubits are accurate and efficient, facilitating better performance of quantum algorithms.

Interference Shield

By incorporating silver into the shielding materials around qubits and their circuitry, quantum computers can achieve a more stable environment that supports a more reliable quantum state.

As quantum computing grows more sophisticated and practical, the demand for materials supporting qubit operation will increase.

Crypto Mining

If you are unfamiliar with how mining works, here's a quick breakdown:

Crypto miners participate in a giant, complex puzzle competition in which everyone tries to solve the same puzzle as quickly as possible. Rather than assembling a picture of a countryside,

these puzzles are complicated math problems solved by elabo-
rate computer networks.

Why do miners participate in these puzzles?

Two reasons:

First, it creates new cryptocurrency coins.

Second, it helps secure the crypto network by verifying the
legitimacy of transactions, ensuring trustworthiness.

As a reward for being the first to solve the puzzle, miners
receive a small amount of cryptocurrency.

So, now you can see the big picture: complicated math
problems solved by supercomputers operating at very high
speeds.

What's the number one enemy of a computer?

Heat.

One of the primary challenges in crypto mining is managing
the immense heat generated by mining rigs.

Silver's excellent thermal conductivity makes it ideal for use
in heat dissipation components such as thermal pastes and heat
sinks. These components are essential for maintaining optimal
operating temperatures and enhancing mining hardware's
efficiency and lifespan. Without adequate heat management,
the processors could overheat, leading to reduced performance
and a shortened lifespan of the entire system.

When it comes to crypto mining, speed and efficiency result
in monetary gain, which means people are willing to allocate
resources to obtain the best equipment.

These sophisticated mining operations are getting increasingly intricate and essential to the ever-evolving landscape
of finance. I know it's still in its infancy, but cryptocurrency is
already reshaping the global financial system.

Cryptocurrency is poised to grow even larger and become
more entrenched in the future of finance and investment.

At the heart of this growing revolution is crypto mining, which drives the demand for cutting-edge electronics and advanced materials. As the industry expands, the need for superior technology will only intensify, solidifying crypto mining's role in shaping tomorrow's financial landscape.

Space Exploration

Space is the final frontier.

In the next decade, we will start dedicating more resources to exploring space and the outer limits of our solar system.

Between companies offering trips to suborbital space and claims from the world's wealthiest people that we need to colonize Mars, there is a strong desire to explore the great unknown.

While exciting from a scientific point of view, the opportunity created by this burgeoning industry will add more pressure on the silver market.

Here's a quick look at how silver will become integral to future space missions and necessary for habitats beyond Earth's boundaries:

Electrical Conductivity

Silver's outstanding electrical conductivity makes it ideal for critical spacecraft components like electrical connectors, wiring, and circuitry. Reliable and efficient electrical connections ensure that essential systems, from navigation to life support, operate without interruption.

Antimicrobial Properties for Hygiene

One lesser-discussed but equally critical challenge of long-duration space missions is managing microbial growth within the spacecraft and controlled environments. Maintaining hygiene is crucial to prevent the spread of bacteria and other microbes. Silver's natural antimicrobial properties make it ideal for coating surfaces and integrating into air filtration systems to safeguard astronauts and prevent microbial growth.

Protection Against Heat and Radiation

Spacecraft protective coatings often include silver due to its excellent reflective properties. These coatings reflect solar radiation away from the spacecraft, protecting it from overheating and minimizing radiation exposure to the electronics and crew.

Communication Systems

Communication is a lifeline in space missions. Silver can enhance the performance of antennas and other communication devices used in space. These silver-enhanced components help achieve more precise and reliable signal transmission and reception, which is critical for routine and emergency transmissions.

Long-term Habitation

Silver's role could expand significantly as space agencies and private companies look towards long-term habitation of other planets. Its antimicrobial properties would be crucial in maintaining sterile environments where the risk of illness needs to be minimized. Additionally, silver helps integrate advanced systems into these habitats, and it is utilized in everything from life support systems to energy solutions.

Thermal Regulation in the Vacuum of Space

Managing space's extreme temperatures is critical for the survival of both crew and equipment. Silver's high thermal conductivity is utilized in components like radiators and heat exchangers aboard spacecraft. These systems rely on silver to effectively dissipate heat generated by onboard equipment and maintain a stable temperature inside the craft.

Water Purification

Another critical use of silver in space is maintaining a clean water supply. Silver is a disinfectant used in Russian Mir and International Space Station water purification systems. It ensures that the water recycled and consumed in space is free from harmful microorganisms, essential for long-duration missions.

If we pursue life in extraterrestrial environments and advance human capabilities beyond Earth, silver will ensure essential technologies operate efficiently in harsh space conditions, keeping future explorers safe and healthy.

Augmented Reality / Virtual Reality

Whether you believe in this technology or not, it has significant support from some of the world's largest companies, so it could either explode in popularity or disappear altogether.

If the former happens, the silver market better watch out because it's used in the critical components of the display systems.

Silvered Mirrors in AR Systems

Silver plays a critical role in forming the partially silvered, semitransparent mirrors that reflect virtual images into the user's field of vision while simultaneously allowing light from the real world to pass through. Silver ensures the mirrors have high reflectivity and durability while maintaining clarity in the visual overlay of augmented reality.

Silver Nanoparticles

Silver nanowires, derived from silver nanoparticles, are increasingly favored over traditional materials

DID YOU KNOW:
The global Virtual Reality market was valued at $23.18 billion in 2023 and is expected to increase to $233.79 billion by the end of 2033.[59]

As of 2023, there are 65.9 million VR users in the United States, with an estimated 171 million VR users worldwide.[60]

because they provide superior conductivity, flexibility, and transparency. These properties are advantageous for AR applications

---

59   https://www.factmr.com/report/virtual-reality-market
60   https://userway.org/blog/virtual-reality-experience/

where display flexibility and durability are essential for user interaction and wearability.

Will Augmented Reality make its way into our daily lives? TV and Movies sure make it seem like it's inevitable, but only time will tell.

One technology that is moving from science fiction to mainstream reality is robotics.

Advanced Robotics

It is an exciting area, with companies like Boston Dynamics, Figure AI, and Tesla building robots and expanding their capabilities.

Elon Musk recently said:

> *'Tesla could start selling its humanoid Optimus robot by the end of next year'*[61]

Companies like Amazon are already replacing workers in their warehouses with robots built by Agility Robotics. "Agility Robotics has targeted the warehousing industry with two-legged bots and sees them eventually stocking shelves and working in hospitals."[62]

The futuristic technology, once contained in the pages of science fiction books, has entered our everyday lives.

If the trend of automation and robotics continues, it will create another demand stream that constantly pressures the silver supply.

---

61   https://www.forbes.com/sites/roberthart/2024/06/14/elon-musk-says-teslas-optimus-robot-could-drive-company-to-25-trillion-valuation-heres-what-experts-think/
62   https://www.bloomberg.com/news/articles/2024-03-04/amazon-warehouses-provide-glimpse-of-workplace-humanoid-robots

In robotics, silver is pivotal in creating more interactive and adaptive machines.

Silver composites allow for the creation of sensors and circuits that can stretch and flex along the robot's body, enhancing its sensory and response capabilities.

Silver's remarkable properties allow companies to push the boundaries, innovate, and experiment in environments where traditional electronic materials would fail.

They can also create more versatile and safer robots that can perform tasks in environments inaccessible to traditional robots.

With all the innovation in the industry, I want to highlight the most interesting and exciting use of silver in robotics.

Silver-Hydrogel

The development of silver-hydrogel composite has marked a significant advancement in robotics. This material combines silver's high electrical conductivity with hydrogels' flexibility and moisture-retaining properties.

Silver-hydrogel has been the key to the advances in robotics over the past few years.

It has allowed scientists to develop better control and responsiveness, closely mimicking natural limb movement and nerve tissue.

The implications and possibilities of this technology extend well beyond the limits of robotics and could have a lasting impact on the entire medical community.

While the robotic advancements are incredible, the innovation and creativity of this industry could be life-changing.

As this field evolves, silver will play an increasingly central role in developing robots capable of performing tasks in previously unimaginable ways.

5G Networks & The Internet of Things

The final emerging technology reshaping our world is the rapidly growing area of 5G networks and the growing popularity of the Internet of Things (IoT).

Let's face it: we live in a connected world, and everything from our lights and thermostats to our beds and toothbrushes is on the internet.

Our world is more connected and automated than ever, and new technology demands more wireless speed, network capacity, and better connectivity—5 G Networks make it all possible.

What is 5G?

5G stands for "fifth generation" wireless technology.

The newest generation of wireless networks boasts:

- Increased Speed
- Greater Capacity
- Reduced Latency

Companies rely on silver in their antennas, switches, and critical network components to ensure speed and reliability. Silver is essential for maintaining a functional network and transmitting data quickly.

SECRET SILVER
Hygienic Door Handles
Step through doors safely with handles coated in Agion silver, designed to kill bacteria from touch and ensure a cleaner, safer environment. How does it work? When an individual touches the door, moisture from their hands activates the release of silver ions, which attach to and eliminate bacteria, resulting in a cleaner handle.

Edge Computing

As data processing shifts closer to the data source rather than centralized data centers, silver helps increase bandwidth and enable real-time data analysis, which is necessary for advanced applications like autonomous driving and smart cities.

The biggest demand for computing power is the massive demand the Internet of Things requires for connectivity.

The Internet of Things

Billions of physical devices worldwide are now connected to the Internet, collecting and sharing data, and this number is set to expand exponentially.

Silver is critical to managing large data volumes and efficiently communicating between devices.

Our world is becoming increasingly connected, and the infrastructure needed to handle the data needs to be built and maintained. This connectivity goes beyond smart devices connected to a home network. The Internet of Things incorporates large-scale, industrial uses like monitoring manufacturing processes, real-time tracking of goods and machinery, smart grids, and urban infrastructure management.

This growing sector will transform society, unlocking groundbreaking opportunities and innovations across multiple industries.

This technological evolution will demand a smarter, more connected future, and that demand will only be fulfilled if we have natural resources like silver to aid in the transition.

The future needs seamless operation and maximum transmission bandwidth for continuous data flow.

Silver is Progress

As an industry insider, I view this trade as a bet on the future—a bet that technology will advance and tomorrow will be better than today. The expanding applications for silver suggest that supply and demand will soon hit a tipping point, likely resulting in a rapid and substantial increase in the metal's price.

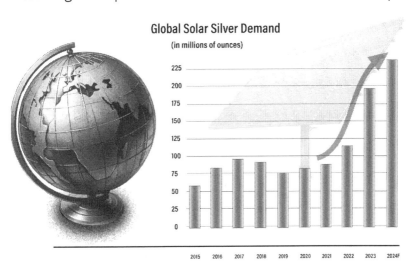

Global Solar Silver Demand
(in millions of ounces)

When will that happen?
I don't know.
But I know it's coming.

As technology becomes ever more integrated into our daily lives, silver will emerge as an essential commodity, much like oil. Silver's unique properties, including its unmatched conductivity and durability, make it vital to the devices and systems defining modern living.

From the smartphones in our pockets to the infrastructure supporting our connected world, silver will be everywhere. It will ensure that we can maintain and elevate our quality of life in a highly digital age. For anyone betting on progress, silver stands out as an investment in the future.

PART 5
Additional Forces Impacting Silver Market Dynamics

The Fight For Access

As nations recognize silver's strategic value, the race to control deposits and secure global supply chains will intensify. Limited availability and rising dependence are likely to make silver a focal point of geopolitical tensions.

Silver is essential to rapidly expanding green technologies, such as solar energy and electronics, and its control may soon become as geopolitically significant as oil once was.

In a world where silver's necessity and status are on the rise, it's easy to envision scenarios of:

- International conflicts over control of deposits
- Heightened tensions around mining rights
- Strategic alliances facilitating trade
- Military interventions and aid to protect silver reserves

Countries rich in silver, such as Mexico and Peru, may find themselves at the center of these tensions. Given their current political instabilities, any external pressures could heighten conflicts.

The likely aggressors?

Nations urgently seeking new sources to protect the development of their technological futures.

These conflicts won't be limited to military action. Economic warfare—through tariffs, sanctions, and trade restrictions—may also be deployed, and it could further destabilize international markets.

For investors, staying informed about silver's geopolitical dynamics is essential. Monitoring these global shifts allows for resilient, forward-thinking strategies that account for potential market impacts.

Strategic positioning will be crucial in navigating this new landscape where silver takes center stage.

Lack of Supply Will
Drive Up Prices

While silver's rising demand has been our focus, we must also address the reality of its steadily decreasing supply.

The supply side is just as critical to silver's price structure. Recent data reveals that production isn't increasing, creating a supply dynamic that directly amplifies silver's price sensitivity.

The Silver Institute reported, "Mine production fell in 2022 to 822.4 million ounces. Production from primary silver mines was almost flat year-on-year, rising by just 0.1 percent to 228.2 Moz." [63]

They further noted, "In 2023, global mined silver production is expected to fall by 2% year-on-year to 820 Moz, driven by lower output from operations in Mexico and Peru. Production from Mexico is expected to fall by 16 Moz."[64]

These figures reflect broader industry challenges: resource depletion and the rising difficulty of extracting silver. The downward trend proves we have a tightening supply amid rising global demand, and we're likely to see rapid price increases.

Sustainable mining practices are also placing further strain on the limited silver supply.

---

63   https://www.silverinstitute.org/mine-production/
64   https://www.silverinstitute.org/mine-production/

As environmental concerns grow, increased industry scrutiny will increase companies' costs and impact the feasibility of mining operations. Add regulatory shifts, government policies, safety concerns, and worker demands, and these factors could soon lead to stricter regulations and higher production costs, ultimately squeezing the silver supply chain.

A regulatory bottleneck could further choke the silver supply, slowing production and pushing prices even higher.

The silver market is at a pivotal juncture. Production is already struggling to keep pace with demand, and further pressures from governments or environmental groups will tip the supply-demand balance in favor of early investors. Given silver's price sensitivity, it only takes a few key mines going offline to create a ripple effect in public markets.

How To Take Action

While financial markets are influenced by factors beyond our control, one thing you *can* control is your choice to invest and strategically position yourself to seize the opportunity.

If you share my view on silver's potential, you're likely wondering how to get started. In the next chapter, I'll share straightforward strategies for entering the silver market so you can maximize this opportunity and grow your wealth.

PART 6
An Insider's Guide to Mastering the Silver Market

The Smart Money Silver Slingshot

While this section moves away from our focus on silver's growing demand and innovative applications, I decided to include it because it offers a valuable perspective on market analysis. As a retail investor, having a diverse toolkit is important, and this information will enhance your ability to navigate the silver market effectively.

This section will introduce you to the Gold/Silver Ratio.

This isn't just a number—it's a way to gauge the market and make more informed investment decisions.

The Gold/Silver Ratio

If there's one thing smart money—AKA institutional investors—love, it's numbers that can be charted, tracked, and studied for a potential edge in the financial markets.

That's how the gold/silver ratio was born.

It's a ratio that measures the ounces of silver needed to purchase one ounce of gold. Investors and analysts use this ratio to gauge the relative value of these two precious metals and make buying and selling decisions.

Understanding the Gold/Silver Ratio

The ratio is calculated by dividing the price of gold per ounce by the price of silver per ounce.

For example, if gold is priced at $2,000 per ounce and silver is at $25 per ounce, the ratio would be 80:1.

$2000/$25 = 80

It would take 80 ounces of silver to buy one ounce of gold.

The ratio fluctuates. Over the last century, it has gone as low as 15:1 and as high as over 100:1.

Here is a monthly look at the chart from 2004 to the present.

Numerous factors influence the ratio.

Economic Conditions

During uncertain times, gold often becomes a refuge for investors, driving its price up relative to silver. Conversely, economic booms tend to boost silver, which is heavily used in industrial applications.

Industrial Demand for Silver

The demand for silver in industries like electronics and solar panels directly impacts its price and, consequently, the gold-to-silver ratio.

Monetary Policies

Changes in interest rates or inflation impact gold more significantly, often causing shifts in the ratio.

Mining Output

Any significant change in the output of gold or silver mines can alter the balance, affecting the ratio.

A Guide to Using the Ratio

Understanding the ratio is one thing. Using it to profit and help guide your investments is another. Here are a few ways institutional investors use this ratio to assist with their investment decisions:

Learn Historical Norms

Familiarize yourself with the historical average of the ratio. Traditionally, if the ratio is higher than the historical average, silver is undervalued relative to gold. Conversely, a below-average ratio indicates that gold is undervalued relative to silver.

Identify Extremes

Look for extreme deviations in the ratio. When the ratio reaches historically high levels, it may be an excellent time to buy silver, as it suggests silver is cheap relative to gold. When the ratio is low, it might be a good time to buy gold, as it suggests gold is cheap relative to silver.

Make Contrarian Investments

If you believe the ratio will revert to the mean, you might buy the undervalued metal (silver when the ratio is high, gold when the ratio is low) and sell the overvalued metal.

Diversify and Hedge

Use the ratio to diversify your holdings between gold and silver. When one is expensive relative to the other, consider reallocating some profits to the undervalued metal.

Example Investment

Suppose the historical average of the gold/silver ratio is around 60:1, but the current ratio stands at 80:1. This suggests that silver is relatively cheap compared to gold. An investor should view this as an opportunity to purchase silver with the view that the silver prices will increase.

On the other hand, if the ratio drops to 40:1, indicating that gold is relatively cheap compared to silver. In that case, an investor should consider this an opportunity to purchase gold as it is relatively inexpensive.

As an investor, you want to pay attention and identify which metal will see a price move to bring the ratio back within historical norms. **When silver is undervalued, its price can slingshot up**.

While this ratio is not a stand-alone method for making investment decisions, when combined with other tools and due diligence, it can help you make more informed choices and potentially enhance your returns.

Now that we've explored this analytical tool, let's focus on a more tangible aspect of silver investing. Many investors, particularly those new to precious metals, wonder about the practicalities of owning physical silver. In the following section, we'll explore the various ways you can physically invest in silver, from coins and bars to ETFs and mining stocks, helping you understand the pros and cons of each approach.

How To Invest In Silver

When investing in silver, tangible assets like coins and bullion offer the most direct and secure way to capitalize on its value.

Owning physical silver offers a sense of ownership and stability that paper assets simply can't match. This section explores various silver investment options, helping you choose the best approach to secure your long-term financial goals.

Coins

Bullion Coins

Coins made from investment-grade silver.

The most popular are **sovereign bullion coins**—minted and guaranteed by government mints. These coins have a face value—even though their silver content makes them worth much more. Sovereign bullion coins are a trusted, stable investment backed by national governments, ensuring both authenticity and long-term value.

Rounds

Privately minted silver rounds offer a lower-premium alternative to sovereign coins. They have no face value and no government backing, so it's essential to confirm purity (at least 0.999% pure silver) for each purchase.

Numismatic coins

AKA rare coins.
Numismatic coins are not recommended for beginner investors due to several challenges they present to newcomers in the market. First, seasoned collectors actively compete for these coins, creating a challenging environment for inexperienced buyers. Rare coins often carry premiums that novice investors might unknowingly pay, potentially leading to overpayment. The value of numismatic coins is based on complex factors such as rarity, condition, and demand, which can be challenging for beginners to gauge and price appropriately.

If your goal is to accumulate a substantial amount of silver, doing so through rare coins is inefficient and complicated.

Investing in numismatic coins is more comparable to buying art than stocks, requiring specialized knowledge that most new investors don't possess. For these reasons, beginners should stick with investment-grade coins whose value is based on silver content. These are more straightforward and directly tied to the price of silver, making them a safer and more efficient choice for building silver holdings without the risks associated with rare coin investing.

Junk Silver

The term "junk silver" is misleading.

Far from worthless, these coins hold significant value due to their silver content. They include U.S. quarters, dimes, Morgan dollars, and Franklin half dollars minted in 1964 or earlier.

Before 1965, U.S. coins like quarters, dimes, and half dollars were minted with genuine silver, giving them **90% silver content**. This significant silver composition means their worth far exceeds their face value, making them an affordable and practical way to acquire silver.

AMOUNT	COIN	FACE VALUE	OUNCES OF SILVER
HOW MANY COINS EQUAL AN OUNCE OF SILVER?			
3	pre-1965 half dollars	$1.50	1
6	pre-1965 quarters	$1.50	1
14	pre-1965 dimes	$1.40	1

Why's it called "Junk Silver?"

The term originated among dealers and collectors to distinguish these common-date coins from rarer, collectible pieces.

I've heard some fascinating stories throughout my career advising clients on precious metal investments. One story about junk silver stands out:

A long-time client of mine had been collecting junk silver for years. He kept his collection in a large glass jar on his bookshelf, just sitting in plain sight.

One night, his home was burglarized. The thieves ransacked the house, looking for the usual targets—laptops, tablets, and jewelry. They rummaged through his desk, drawers, and even his bathroom and stole everything that had even a little bit of value, but they didn't touch the massive jar of coins.

The burglars left almost ten thousand dollars of silver untouched because they assumed it was loose change and not worth the effort!

The irony of thieves frantically grabbing old computers yet ignoring the most valuable item in the house is not only amusing but also serves as a powerful metaphor for the overlooked potential of silver investment. Sometimes, the most significant opportunities are those that others fail to recognize.

Bullion Bars

Bullion bars, which range in size from 1 oz to 1,000 oz, are an efficient way to accumulate large amounts of silver.

Exchange Traded Funds

Exchange-traded funds can be bought and sold like stocks, providing liquidity and flexibility to investors, and are often touted as a simple way to invest in silver. They offer investors a convenient method to gain exposure to metal markets without holding physical silver.

While ETFs offer convenience, they have drawbacks that investors should consider carefully.

Lack of transparency: The actual silver holdings of ETF custodians are often unclear, relying solely on their reporting.

No physical redemption: Unlike owning physical silver, ETF shares can't be exchanged for actual metal, negating a key benefit of silver ownership.

Counterparty risk: Your investment depends on the financial stability and honesty of fund managers, custodians, and other parties.

Imperfect price tracking: Management fees, trading costs, and other factors can cause ETFs to diverge from silver's price.

Given these limitations, owning physical silver directly—or storing it in private storage— provides greater security and control over your investment.

Direct ownership gives you complete control over your investment without relying on third parties. Physical ownership eliminates the risks associated with the financial stability of fund managers or custodians. Physical ownership also offers more privacy than ETF investments, which leave a paper trail.

Plus, you can quickly sell or use your physical silver as needed without going through financial intermediaries.

Options and Futures Trading

Options and futures are liquid markets where you can trade to take advantage of short-term price movements. This extremely sophisticated strategy requires understanding derivatives markets and an appetite for higher risk.

Silver Funds

Funds that invest in silver mining companies, indirectly exposing you to silver prices. As silver prices rise, mining revenue increases, benefiting the fund.

Individual Mining Stocks

Direct investment in silver mining companies offers an alternative to Silver Funds but has its own considerations. Mining stocks are influenced by factors beyond silver prices, including company performance, management decisions, operational challenges, environmental regulations, and geopolitical risks.

By investing in miners, you're essentially backing a business operation rather than owning the metal itself. Ultimately, investing in miners means investing in a business, with all the complexities and opportunities that entails, rather than simply tracking the price of silver.

Silver IRA

For those interested in adding silver to retirement plans, a Silver IRA provides tax-deferred growth with the security of physical silver assets.

A self-directed IRA gives you the flexibility to diversify beyond traditional investments and into physical precious metals, bringing tax-deferred growth potential to your silver holdings. Your silver investment is safely secured in an IRS-approved depository, combining the security of physical assets with the tax benefits of a retirement account.

Here's what makes a Silver IRA powerful:

- Tax-deferred growth potential
- Easy transfers from existing retirement accounts (IRAs, 401(k)s)
- Professional storage in secure, IRS-approved facilities
- Complete control over your investment decisions
- Protection through physical precious metals

Noble Gold Investments understands that navigating retirement options can feel overwhelming. That's why they've streamlined the process of setting up your Silver IRA, offering personalized, stress-free solutions and guidance every step of the way. Their expertise ensures you can confidently diversify your retirement portfolio with precious metals while maximizing growth potential and minimizing risk.

About Noble Gold Investments

As a precious metals broker with extensive experience in the industry, I understand the importance of determining what's best for your investment goals and matching investment vehicles to individual needs.

Noble Gold Investments has over $2 billion in sales and is trusted by thousands of investors. This level of success and trust comes from our commitment to making it easy and safe for investors to navigate the complexities of the precious metals market.

At Noble Gold Investments, our associates are ready to help you make informed decisions about your precious metals investments.

We offer two flagship services designed to cater to different investor preferences and needs:

Silver IRA

When you open a Silver IRA, it is established as a Self-Directed IRA. A Self-Directed IRA is a retirement account under the investor's control that can hold precious metals, such as physical silver bars and coins.

With a Self-Directed IRA, you have complete control of your precious metals.

Adding silver or other precious metals to your current IRA is simple and hassle-free.

You can transfer your entire IRA, or just a portion of it, into a new Self-Directed Silver IRA. This common practice is called a "Direct Rollover" or a "Direct Transfer." It is a tax-free transaction, meaning the IRS allows you to move funds out of one IRA into another IRA free of tax penalties.

Many individuals also have old 401(k) accounts or other types of retirement plans from previous employers, such as a 403(b), 457(b), Thrift Savings Plan, annuity, or pension plan. By requesting a rollover, these plans can be converted tax-free into a Silver IRA.

In most instances, a simple phone call will allow the current custodian of your 401(k) plan to release those funds directly into your new Silver IRA.

On the other hand, if you'd prefer to keep your precious metals closer to home, we also offer the option to have your silver shipped safely and discreetly to your doorstep.

Silver Delivered To Your Doorstep

From picking up your phone and placing the order to our delivery partner dropping it off at your doorstep, we have perfected our process so your transaction is easy and enjoyable.

What Makes Noble Gold Investments Special

At Noble Gold Investments, we pride ourselves on being more than just another precious metals company. We've built our reputation on trust, education, and unparalleled customer service.

We specialize in helping individuals like you diversify their portfolios with the most reliable and historically proven assets—gold and silver.

We're dedicated to empowering you with the knowledge and tools to protect and grow your wealth, regardless of market conditions.

We prioritize our clients' peace of mind, ensuring every investment meets your unique financial goals with total transparency and flexibility.

We take a personalized approach, tailoring strategies to meet your unique financial goals.

I founded Noble Gold Investments to address the four key areas important to every investor: customer service, security, costs, and a buyback program.

Allow me to walk you through our solutions to these industry-wide problems:

Elite Customer Service

We've built an industry-leading, end-to-end white-glove concierge service for all our clients.

Your value and treatment are not based on dollar amount—every client receives the same high-level attention and service. Our team of experienced, US-based associates is dedicated to delivering top-tier service, whether you're investing $5,000 or $5 million. This commitment means you'll always reach a dedicated professional—ready to assist and answer all your questions directly. No automated systems, no long hold times—just real help when you need it.

You call. We answer.

You have questions. We have answers.

Uncompromising Security

Your security is our primary concern, and we go above and beyond to ensure your precious metals receive the highest level of protection at every stage. From secure, fully insured shipping right to your doorstep to safeguarding your assets in our secure depository, we prioritize safety and privacy.

Our team implements industry-leading best practices, including strict chain-of-custody protocols, advanced tracking systems, and secure handling procedures. These measures guarantee every aspect of your precious metals ownership is protected, allowing you to rest assured.

Low Fees

We offer the most competitive fee structure in the industry. I heard a common complaint about the exorbitant fees charged by the industry's more prominent players. Our mission is to provide some of the best fees in the market, making our services accessible to everyone striving for financial stability.

Our commitment to fair pricing ensures complete transparency—no hidden costs, no surprises.

Guaranteed Buyback Program

Your investment is only as good as your ability to liquidate it when the time comes. That's why we've built one of the most robust buyback programs in the precious metals industry. When you buy precious metals from us, we guarantee we'll repurchase them when you're ready to liquidate.

When you need your money, you need it now—not in 6 months, and certainly not at a devalued rate that takes advantage of you. That's why we've made selling precious metals easier than buying them.

Our commitment to addressing these core issues has led to remarkable success. We've been voted the number one gold IRA company for four years running and have completed over $2 billion in sales.

But what I'm most proud of is that we have one of the highest percentages of repeat customers in the business. This tells me that we exceed expectations and build lasting relationships based on trust, satisfaction, and a commitment to our clients' financial success.

At Noble Gold Investments, we believe in building relationships based on honesty, transparency, and trust—not on gimmicky offers, inflated fees, or high-pressure sales tactics.

Investing in precious metals is already challenging enough. We want your transaction to be easy, safe, and worry-free.

It only takes 5 minutes to get started, and the payoff will last a lifetime.

Secure your future with a trusted silver investment.

SECTION TWO

SEEKING R.O.I.

(Rogue Opportunities and Investments)

PART 1
My Investment Philosophy

Redefining the Investment Process

In today's world, conformity and mediocrity are not just accepted—they're celebrated and rewarded.

Conventional wisdom says to play it safe, follow the crowd, and stick to the beaten path. But this approach often leads to missed opportunities and, at best, average results.

In the following pages, I'll share the principles and strategies that have guided my investment journey and formed the backbone of my philosophy: **Rogue Opportunities and Investments.**

Whether you're an experienced investor or just starting, I want to equip you with the knowledge and insights to break free from the ordinary and achieve the extraordinary.

Welcome to the rogue path—a journey where we defy convention, embrace opportunity, and build lasting wealth on our terms.

Rogue Opportunities and Investments Ethos

I believe in defying conventional wisdom to seize untapped opportunities. My philosophy centers on owning tangible assets, taking calculated risks, and acting decisively on deep market insights.

I focus on building wealth through strategic, high-conviction investments in overlooked markets while staying ahead of the curve.

By thinking differently, acting independently, and moving swiftly, you can create your path to success.

Why I Chose An Alternative Path To Wealth Generation

My financial epiphany came when I realized:

The financial industry serves itself first and its clients second.

Years of modest returns and high fees led me to question everything.

Why settle for a 5% return when opportunities for 20%, 30%, or even more exist?

Why limit myself to public markets when private deals offer greater potential?

The first lesson I learned was to question every assumption.

This shift in mindset led me to reexamine all the financial notions I'd simply accepted because they were widely parroted and seemed accurate on the surface.

Is what they say true, or does it sound convincing
because you haven't taken the time to
dive deeper and stress-test it?

Mainstream financial advice often preaches diversification, dollar-cost averaging, and passive index investing. While these strategies may protect against catastrophic loss, they also ensure mediocre returns.

What's the fun in mediocre returns?

Why take on risk for a mediocre return?

Mediocre is average.

My goal isn't to be average—and I'm guessing yours isn't either.

Average gets lost in the crowd. I want to stand out, be the best I can be, and create something I am proud of.

A pivotal moment came during the 2008 financial crisis. While many saw devastation, I saw opportunity.

As the bottom fell out of the real estate market, I took a risk and purchased a distressed commercial property. By acquiring a distressed property, I multiplied my wealth in the following years.

Where others saw fear, I saw potential.

The result?

I was rewarded with an asymmetrical investment—the upside far outweighed the downside risk.

Had I followed the crowd, I would have watched from the sidelines as one of the most incredible real estate opportunities passed me by.

That experience taught me an important lesson: **true wealth is built by those who think and act independently of the herd**.

Over the next decade, I developed a framework for investing success.

Prepare for a deep dive into my playbook of investing principles, carefully crafted from years of experience.

Innovation and progress come from those
willing to challenge the status quo.

Principles of R.O.I.

The philosophy I developed has guided me through turbulent market cycles and now serves as the foundation for every financial opportunity I pursue. Hands-on experience, keen observation, and a willingness to challenge conventional wisdom forged these ten principles.

Tenets of My Investing & Wealth-Building Plan

- **Tangible Assets**
- **Focused Investment**
- **Strategic Diversification**
- **Alternative Assets**
- **Calculated & Controlled Risk-Taking**
- **Mindset & Emotional Intelligence**
- **Spotting Opportunities**
- **Decisive Action**
- **Mastering Market Dynamics**
- **Thinking Differently**

Let's dive into each principle so you can build your investing framework and develop your decision-making ability.

Tangible Assets

First and foremost, owning tangible assets—real estate, business inventory, equipment, or precious metals—is superior to investing in stocks and companies you can't control.

When you own an asset, you have the power to influence its success, make strategic decisions, and directly benefit from its growth. This level of control and involvement is something traditional investments can't offer.

Tangible assets provide security and stability, often lacking in the volatile world of stocks and bonds. They are physical and concrete and have intrinsic value that isn't subject to the whims of market sentiment or corporate mismanagement.

Real estate can be improved, rented out, or developed to enhance its value. Similarly, owning precious metals like gold and silver hedges against inflation and economic uncertainty and offers a form of wealth that has stood the test of time.

Tangible assets often present income generation and appreciation opportunities that are more predictable and within your control. Whether collecting rental income from real estate, generating revenue from business equipment, or benefitting from the increasing demand for commodities, these assets work for you in a way that passive stock ownership cannot.

During economic downturns, tangible assets hold their value better than intangible investments. While the stock markets can crash and companies fail, tangible assets often retain value, providing a financial cushion and a source of potential liquidity when needed most.

Tangible assets offer a unique combination of control, stability, and long-term growth potential.

Focusing on these physical investments can build a more resilient and secure financial future.

Focused Investment

Focused investments are the key to creating wealth. By concentrating your efforts on a few high-potential opportunities, you maximize your returns and build value.

When you focus your investments, you allocate your resources—time, money, and energy—toward opportunities you understand and have firm conviction.

This concentrated approach allows you to dive deep into the specifics of each investment, gaining knowledge of the market, the asset, and the factors that drive its success. This depth of understanding gives you an edge that's hard to achieve when your attention is spread across too many investments.

Focused investing also means putting more of your capital to work in areas where you see the most significant potential for growth. Instead of spreading your investments across a wide range of assets or sectors, you hone in on the few that offer the most promise. This concentrated bet can lead to outsized returns, especially when you've done your homework and are confident in the underlying fundamentals of the investment.

This approach contrasts sharply with the more traditional method of diversification, which often involves spreading risk across many different investments to minimize potential losses. **While diversification is a valuable strategy for preserving wealth, it can dilute your potential gains in the early stages.**

By trying to avoid losses, you limit your upside. Focused investing embraces the idea that taking calculated risks on a few well-chosen opportunities can yield far greater rewards.

Another advantage of focused investment is the ability to be agile and responsive. With fewer investments, you can more easily monitor each one, making adjustments to optimize performance. This agility allows you to capitalize on opportunities and mitigate risks more effectively than juggling an extensive, diverse portfolio.

Focused investing requires a disciplined mindset. It demands that you resist the temptation to chase every new trend or investment idea that comes your way. Instead, you must commit to your chosen focus areas, continuously refining your knowledge and staying the course even when market conditions become challenging.

Focused investments are about quality over quantity.

By concentrating your resources on high-potential areas, you position yourself to create significant wealth.

Strategic Diversification

After wealth is created, diversification becomes necessary. Spreading your investments across various assets helps maintain and protect what you've built, offering a buffer against market volatility and unforeseen challenges.

Strategic diversification involves allocating investments across various asset classes and sectors to safeguard wealth. While focused investments build substantial value, diversification preserves and sustains that value over the long term.

The rationale behind diversification is simple: minimize the impact of any investment's poor performance on your overall portfolio.

Market conditions can change rapidly and unpredictably, and what was once a high-performing asset may face downturns due to economic shifts, regulatory changes, or other unforeseen factors. Diversification spreads your exposure across different investments so that a decline in one area doesn't significantly erode your overall wealth.

Strategic diversification goes beyond random asset allocation. It's a thoughtful approach that selects investments to balance and complement each other. The goal is to create a portfolio where assets respond differently to various market conditions—some thriving during economic booms, others providing stability in downturns.

For example, combining tangible assets like precious metals with alternative investments such as private equity or commodities can create a portfolio well-positioned to weather all market cycles.

Strategic diversification means you understand the correlation between your investments.

Highly correlated assets tend to move in the same direction under similar conditions, which can increase your risk exposure.

Diversification is not a set-it-and-forget-it strategy. It requires ongoing assessment and rebalancing to ensure your portfolio is aligned with your long-term objectives.

Remember:

Focus builds wealth. Diversification keeps it.

Alternative Assets

Traditional Assets vs Alternative Assets.

My approach is also rooted in the belief that alternative assets offer unique opportunities mainstream investors often overlook. While sometimes riskier, these assets can provide outsized returns if approached with the right strategy.

Traditional assets like bonds and blue-chip stocks offer stability but often have limited upside potential. On the other hand, alternative investments—such as real estate, cryptocurrencies, precious metals, and business ownership—present higher risks and the potential for substantial rewards.

Look at early Bitcoin investors. They recognized potential and invested despite widespread skepticism and were rewarded with returns in the thousands of percent. Those willing to explore uncharted territory and make informed decisions can achieve remarkable success.

However, success in alternative investing requires a deep understanding of the asset class, careful due diligence, and an understanding of risk management.

It's not about chasing the latest trend or mindlessly following the crowd. Alternative assets offer unique growth and protection opportunities often overlooked by the mainstream. This allows you to identify opportunities where the risk-reward profile aligns with your investment goals and risk tolerance.

True wealth is often found off the beaten path, where independent thinking and strategic risk-taking pave the way for success.

Calculated & Controlled Risk-Taking

Taking calculated risks is essential for any investor looking to achieve significant success.

Playing it safe may protect you from losses but also limits your upside.

Understanding when to take risks—and how to mitigate them—is an essential skill in the investor's toolkit.

Risk is an inherent part of investing, but how you approach it can make all the difference.

Calculated risk-taking is not about jumping into every opportunity that comes your way. It's about evaluating the potential rewards against risks and making informed decisions based on thorough analysis and strategic foresight.

This approach allows you to take advantage of opportunities others might overlook due to fear or uncertainty.

Developing a Mindset for Risk

Embracing risk is not about recklessness but recognizing and seizing opportunities where others see obstacles.

The best value is overlooked or misunderstood by the broader market.

This requires a mindset that not only tolerates risk but thrives on it—a mindset that is open to exploring unconventional paths and willing to challenge established norms.

Developing this mindset is crucial for investors who want to stay ahead of the curve. It involves cultivating a sense of when and where to take risks, understanding the broader market context, and being willing to act when opportunities arise.

It's about being proactive rather than reactive.

It's about having the confidence to trust your analysis and judgment even when they go against conventional thinking.

You must develop a mindset that embraces risk as a necessary component of successful investing. It's your job to position yourself to capitalize on opportunities others might shy away from.

Risk-Return Trade-offs

Each asset class carries its own set of risks and potential returns.

To navigate these trade-offs effectively, you must clearly understand your financial objectives and the risks involved in achieving them.

This delicate balance is essential for long-term success in investing.

As an investor, you can not continually take on risk where the downside is more significant than the upside. In the long run, you will lose!

Also, you can not let the downside get away from you. You must be comfortable with reducing risk and protecting yourself.

Mindset & Emotional Intelligence

Emotion plays a significant role in investing, and I've learned that mastering your emotions is vital to making sound decisions.

Fear, greed, and FOMO (Fear Of Missing Out) can cloud judgment, leading to poor choices that undermine your long-term goals.

Successful investors possess the ability to remain calm and rational during market turbulence.

Psychology of Investing

The market is as much a psychological battlefield as a financial one, and the greatest challenges often come from within.

Investors are prone to cognitive biases and emotional responses that can lead to poor decision-making.

Some of the most common psychological traps include:

Confirmation Bias: The tendency to seek information confirming your beliefs while disregarding evidence that contradicts them. This leads to overconfidence in flawed strategies and missed opportunities to correct course.

FOMO (Fear of Missing Out): The fear that others are profiting from an opportunity you're not part of can drive impulsive decisions, often at the worst possible times. Chasing trends can result in buying high and selling low.

Loss Aversion: Studies show we tend to feel losses more strongly than gains—it's human nature. This can make you play it too safe with your money and prevent you from taking the risks necessary to achieve significant returns.

To combat these psychological traps, developing emotional discipline is essential.

Objective Decision-Making: Basing investment decisions on solid, objective analysis rather than emotions or market sentiment. This requires a systematic approach to evaluating opportunities and rational analysis rather than gut feelings.

Courage of Conviction: Having the confidence to act on your well-researched convictions, even when it means going against the crowd. Successful investors are often those who see value where others do not.

Long-Term Perspective: Focusing on your long-term goals and resisting the urge to make reactionary moves based on short-term market fluctuations. Markets are inherently volatile; knee-jerk reactions to daily price movements can derail your investment strategy.

Emotional Discipline

The ability to maintain clarity and discipline in decision-making is what differentiates successful investors from the rest.

Let's examine how you can cultivate emotional discipline.

Creating a Plan and Sticking to It: Establish a clear investment strategy that aligns with your financial goals and risk tolerance. Make decisions consistent with your long-term objectives rather than being swayed by market noise.

Regular Self-Reflection: Assess your emotional state and decision-making processes. Are you reacting out of fear or greed? Self-awareness is crucial in recognizing when emotions are influencing your choices.

Mindfulness and Stress Management: Investing can be stressful, especially during market volatility. Techniques such as meditation, regular exercise, and stress management can help you maintain a calm and focused mind.

Learning from Mistakes: Accept that mistakes are part of the learning process. Rather than letting them erode your confidence, use them as opportunities to refine your strategy and improve your emotional resilience. Analyze past errors without judgment and make adjustments to avoid repeating them.

Mastering your mindset and emotional intelligence is as vital to your investment success as understanding the technical aspects of the market. Cultivating emotional discipline allows you to navigate market fluctuations clearly and confidently, enabling more rational decision-making even in turbulent times.

Spotting Opportunities

Spotting opportunities before they become mainstream is essential for contrarian investors, who thrive by going against the grain and uncovering value where others see none.

Identifying Unique Opportunities

The contrarian investor's edge comes from identifying trends and shifts before they become apparent to the masses.

This foresight allows you to position yourself ahead of the curve, capitalizing on opportunities that others may only recognize once gains have materialized and the risk/reward balance is no longer favorable.

Methods to Spot Opportunities

You need to employ methods that allow you to anticipate where the market is heading:

Trend Analysis: Whether it's a new technology, shifting consumer behaviors, or evolving industry dynamics, understanding these trends early can give you a significant advantage.

Economic Indicators: Monitor data such as inflation rates, employment data, interest rates, and GDP growth closely. These metrics provide insight into the economy's overall health and can signal upcoming shifts in market conditions.

Sociopolitical Changes: Stay informed about global events, regulatory changes, and technological advancements. These factors can create new investment opportunities or introduce risks that could alter the landscape of entire industries.

Staying Ahead of Trends

Maintaining a competitive edge in investing requires staying ahead of trends. This demands a proactive approach to information gathering, analysis, and decision-making.

Understanding the implications of a new technology, consumer behavior, or change in the economic environment could help you identify a groundbreaking investment opportunity before it becomes mainstream.

The opportunistic investor must develop the critical skill of recognizing trend changes, especially those who take a contrarian approach. This proactive, informed approach is key to staying ahead of the curve and achieving long-term success in the ever-evolving investing world.

Decisive Action

Swift decision-making is critical to successful investing, allowing you to capitalize on opportunities before they disappear. In life, timing is everything, and acting quickly and confidently can make the difference between securing a lucrative investment and watching it slip away.

Taking Decisive Action

Spotting opportunities is only half the battle. The real challenge lies in acting on them.

Once you've identified a promising investment, you must move on it quickly. Hesitation leads to missed opportunities.

In fast-moving environments, delays can be costly.

The ability to move decisively comes from confidence, preparation, and the ability to trust your instincts. Confidence comes from thorough research and analysis—knowing that you've done your homework assures you to act swiftly. Preparation involves having a clear strategy and understanding the risks and rewards associated with the opportunity. When you've taken the time to develop a well-informed plan, you're less likely to second-guess yourself in the heat of the moment.

Decisive action doesn't mean acting impulsively or without due diligence. It's about making informed decisions quickly and being willing to take action when the right opportunity arises.

You find the best opportunities where others fear to tread, and your ability to think independently and move decisively gives you a distinct advantage.

Successful investing is often about being in the right place at the right time and being prepared to act when that moment comes.

The most successful investors can cut through the chatter and make bold decisions when the situation calls for it.

Overcoming the Fear of Action

The fear of loss or the anxiety of being wrong can paralyze even the most experienced investors. It's important to recognize that inaction is often riskier than making a bad decision, and sometimes it's even more costly.

To overcome this fear, develop a mindset that accepts the possibility of failure as part of the investment process. No strategy is foolproof, and not every decision will lead to success. The key is to learn from each experience, refine your approach, and continue to move forward.

By embracing the potential for both success and failure, you free yourself from the paralysis of overthinking and allow yourself to take the necessary steps to seize opportunities as they arise.

Consistency in Decisive Action

Decisive action is not a one-time event but a consistent approach to investing.

Cultivating the ability to identify and act on opportunities with confidence sets you apart in the investment world. This skill, combined with thorough preparation and independent thinking, allows you to find value in places where others see only risk.

By developing this eye and the willingness to move decisively, you position yourself to capitalize.

Mastering Market Dynamics

Knowledge is power, and by fully grasping the dynamics of a market, you can capitalize on opportunities when the market becomes disjointed from intrinsic value.

This understanding allows you to identify when to sell in an overvalued market or buy in an undervalued one.

It also enables you to spot gaps in the market—unmet needs or emerging trends—that others have yet to recognize.

A comprehensive grasp of market dynamics gives you an unfair advantage and allows you to make informed decisions that can significantly enhance your investment outcomes.

Strategic Insight and Timing

Mastering market dynamics involves more than just knowing the basics of supply and demand; it requires a nuanced understanding of the factors that drive market behavior.

For instance, understanding the cyclical nature of real estate markets might allow you to buy properties during a downturn when prices are low and sell during a boom when demand drives prices up.

Similarly, recognizing the early signs of a technological disruption could lead you to invest in startups poised to redefine their industries.

Investing in Niche Markets

Niche markets—such as rare collectibles, niche real estate markets like vacation rentals in emerging tourist spots, or specialized commodities—offer unique opportunities often overlooked by traditional investors.

Although these markets may be less understood, they can provide outsized returns for those with the expertise to navigate them.

Recognizing the growth potential in an emerging tourist destination might lead you to invest in vacation rentals before the market becomes saturated. Understanding the increasing demand for a rare commodity could position you to benefit as prices rise.

This one bit of advice has generated millions of dollars!

Concentrating Investments in Areas of Expertise

Concentrating your investments in areas you understand allows you to capitalize on your knowledge and insight, giving you a distinct advantage over generalist investors who lack the same level of expertise.

That alone is a massive competitive edge.

When you focus your investments in markets you understand intimately, you can better anticipate shifts, identify opportunities, and manage risks.

This concentrated approach allows you to leverage your expertise to make more informed decisions and to act with greater confidence.

Concentrating your investments in areas you understand allows you to capitalize on your knowledge and insight, giving you a distinct advantage over generalist investors who lack the same level of expertise.

Staying Ahead of the Curve

To truly master market dynamics, staying ahead of the curve is crucial. This means continuously expanding your knowledge, staying updated on the latest developments in your chosen markets, and adapting your strategy as new information becomes available.

The most successful investors are those who never stop learning and are constantly working to sharpen their edge.

Combining swift decision-making with deep market knowledge gives you an unbeatable edge.

Thinking Differently

Finally, I believe in going against the grain of conventional thinking. Herd mentality leads investors down the wrong path, as following the crowd results in average outcomes.

The willingness to think differently, challenge the status quo, and make bold moves when others are hesitant has allowed me to thrive and build a secure lifestyle and future for my family.

By adopting a contrarian mindset, you can position yourself to succeed where the masses fall short.

Challenging Mainstream Advice

Mainstream financial advice often promotes a one-size-fits-all strategy.

While these principles benefit some, they often produce mediocre results for individuals who aspire to achieve something more substantial.

You should consider what success means to them and how best to achieve it.

One key element of thinking differently is understanding that conventional wisdom is not always wise. Financial tropes like "buy and hold" or "diversify to minimize risk" are often repeated without considering an individual's unique circumstances, goals, or risk tolerance.

While these strategies can be effective, blindly following them can prevent you from seizing higher-risk, higher-reward opportunities that could significantly enhance your wealth.

The path to extraordinary wealth often requires forging your way.

The Power of Independent Thinking

Independent thinking means having the confidence to trust your analysis and judgment.

This doesn't mean rejecting all conventional advice outright but rather questioning its relevance to your situation and being willing to explore alternatives that align with your goals.

Independent thinking also involves recognizing that markets are driven by human behavior, which is often irrational and emotional.

This creates opportunities for those who can remain objective and detached, capitalizing on others' mistakes and overreactions.

Like when the masses panic sell during a market downturn, an independent thinker might see this as a buying opportunity, recognizing that the underlying fundamentals of certain investments remain strong.

Bold Moves in the Face of Uncertainty

Thinking differently also means making bold moves in the face of uncertainty. When executed with careful planning and strategic insight, bold moves lead to outsized returns.

Boldness must be tempered with discipline.

This is not about taking reckless risks but about making informed decisions based on a deep understanding of the market dynamics.

Combining bold action with disciplined analysis gives you confidence and precision.

Building a Strategy for Success

Internalizing these principles allows you to confidently build your own strategy that navigates the complex investment landscape. To do that, you must cultivate a mindset that challenges norms, questions conventional wisdom, and charts its own course in the financial world. By fostering independent thought and embracing bold action, you're not just positioning yourself for success—you're opening doors to extraordinary results, lasting wealth, and a better future for you and your loved ones.

When it comes to investing, thinking differently isn't just an advantage – it's necessary for those who want to excel.

Principles in Practice

The true test of any strategy is its practical application.

What follows is a blueprint for implementing these concepts in your investment journey.

PART 2
Three Unconventional Wealth-Building Strategies

Satellite City Approach

Years ago, while working in commercial real estate, the most frequent request I received from a client was: "Find me a deal."

Everyone wanted undervalued properties with significant appreciation potential. My mentor taught me that rapid appreciation hinged on entering a market just before it heated up.

How do you know if an area is poised for growth?

I developed a strategy I called the "Starbucks Theory."

At the time, Starbucks was known for its heavy investment in research to identify up-and-coming neighborhoods.

My approach? Turn their research into riches.

I scoured the city for new Starbucks locations, particularly those opening on the edges of less desirable areas. Once spotted, I'd guide my clients to nearby properties.

This simple yet powerful indicator helped my clients secure assets in transitioning neighborhoods where others failed to see value. By understanding the market, acting early, and moving swiftly, my clients stayed ahead of the curve, significantly boosting their portfolios as property values soared.

Today, I've scaled up this principle in my investing. Instead of coffee shops, I now track rapidly growing cities as the new opportunity indicator. I focus on areas within a one-hour drive of these booming urban centers—a strategy I call the **Satellite City Approach**.

Investment Theory

Successful investments happen by entering early, not by chasing markets once they've become saturated.

My investment strategy targets smaller cities within a 60-mile radius of expanding metropolitan areas, unlocking benefits such as robust growth potential, attractive afford-ability, and reduced competition. This approach capitalizes on the proximity to major metros, providing access to high-quality services and infrastructure without the hefty price tag associ-ated with larger cities.

By focusing on these strategic locations, investors can leverage the best of both worlds – the economic opportunities of a major urban center and the cost advantages of a smaller market.

These smaller cities sit within a short commute of the larger city's amenities, such as top-tier healthcare, education, entertain-ment, and shopping. This accessibility makes them attractive to residents and businesses looking to enjoy the benefits of a large city without its high cost of living.

By investing early, you position yourself to capi-talize on these smaller cities' natural expansion and growth as they evolve.

DID YOU KNOW: The Global Commercial Real Estate Market Size was valued at USD 7.2 Trillion in 2023, and the Worldwide Commercial Real Estate Market Size is Expected to Reach USD 9.91 Trillion by 2033[65]

---

65 https://finance.yahoo.com/news/global-commercial-real-estate-market-050000139.html

This allows you to acquire lower-priced properties with significant appreciation potential as the city grows.

These smaller cities aren't random; they are proven markets with expansion potential. Their proximity to larger cities means they're already benefiting from spillover effects.

Investing here lets you harness the growth of a larger city in a more manageable—and often more profitable—environment. As these cities grow, they'll attract residents, businesses, and investors, driving up property values and rental rates. By getting in early, you can secure prime assets that will grow as the city develops.

The alternative—chasing markets—often involves entering at the peak when prices are high and the potential for returns is lower. My approach mitigates this risk, as you are not buying into overheated markets, where the upside is limited, and the potential for a downturn is greater.

This method allows me to:

1. Tap into significant growth potential
2. Limit risk
3. Beat the market rush
4. Capitalize on the spillover effect of urban expansion

This strategy isn't about trend-following. It's about trend anticipation and aligns with my principle of seeing opportunities where others don't and acting decisively to capitalize on them.

Investing in satellite cities positions you at the forefront of the next growth wave, just like spotting Starbucks in an up-and-coming neighborhood.

Advantages of the Satellite City Approach

As an investor, this approach gives you several advantages:

Affordability

Property prices are lower in smaller cities, allowing a lower entry point for investors. This affordability can translate into better cash flow from rental properties or reduced acquisition costs in commercial real estate.

Population Growth

As major cities become more expensive, people move to nearby smaller towns, driving up demand for housing, retail, and services. This trend will likely continue, especially as remote work allows greater flexibility in choosing where to live.

Infrastructure Development

Proximity to a major city often means these smaller cities benefit from infrastructure investments like improved highways, public transport extensions, and commercial developments.

Lower Competition

Smaller markets typically face less competition from large institutional investors, allowing for better deals and value-added investment opportunities.

Example Satellite Cities

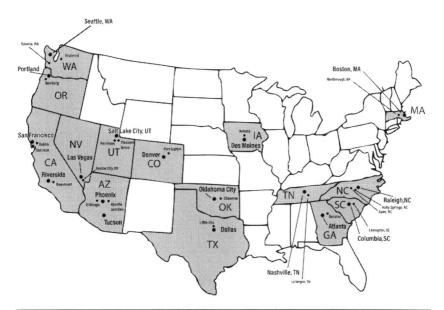

Satellite City	Population	Large City	Population	Miles from Large City	State
Lexington, SC	25,343	Columbia, SC	144,489	15 miles	South Carolina
El Mirage, AZ	35,815	Tucson, AZ	548,772	5 miles	Arizona
La Vergne, TN	39,597	Nashville, TN	712,334	20 miles	Tennessee
Holly Springs, NC	46,271	Raleigh, NC	482,295	20 miles	North Carolina
Fort Lupton, CO	9,447	Denver, CO	716,577	30 miles	Colorado
Boulder City, NV	14,828	Las Vegas, NV	660,929	26 miles	Nevada
Tukwila, WA	21,135	Seattle, WA	755,078	11 miles	Washington
Decatur, GA	24,307	Atlanta, GA	510,823	7 miles	Georgia
Shawnee, OK	31,803	Oklahoma City, OK	702,767	39 miles	Oklahoma
Pleasant Grove, UT	37,294	Salt Lake City, UT	209,593	36 miles	Utah
Newberg, OR	26,095	Portland, OR	630,498	25 miles	Oregon
Apache Junction, AZ	41,153	Phoenix, AZ	1,650,070	37 miles	Arizona
Marlborough, MA	41,179	Boston, MA	653,833	32 miles	Massachusetts
Beaumont, CA	58,463	Riverside, CA	318,858	26 miles	California
Redmond, WA	80,280	Seattle, WA	755,078	16 miles	Washington
Dublin, CA	69,128	San Jose, CA/ San Francisco, CA	969,655/ 808,988	41 miles/ 35 miles	California
Herriman, UT	60,049	Salt Lake City	209,593	25 miles	Utah
Little Elm, TX	58,496	Dallas, TX	1,302,868	33 miles	Texas
Apex, NC	72,225	Raleigh, NC	482,295	15 miles	North Carolina
Ankeny, IA	74,458	Des Moines, IA	210,381	13 miles	Iowa

1. Lexington, SC
Opportunity:

This city's proximity to the state capital of Columbia positions it well for growth, particularly as Columbia continues to expand. Look for residential and commercial opportunities, especially those catering to middle-income families and professionals.

Strategy:

Focus on single-family homes and small multifamily properties. Consider mixed-use developments as well.

2. El Mirage, AZ
Opportunity:

A short distance from Tucson, this city could benefit from the university-driven economy and growing tech sector in Tucson.

Strategy:

Focus on affordable housing and rental units that appeal to students and young professionals.

3. La Vergne, TN
Opportunity:

The ongoing boom in Nashville's real estate market due to its vibrant music and entertainment industry spills over to nearby La Vergne.

Strategy:

Look into multifamily properties and commercial real estate catering to the entertainment industry and related services.

4. Holly Springs, NC

Opportunity:

The Research Triangle in Raleigh is one of the fastest-growing tech hubs in the U.S., making Holly Springs attractive for those priced out of Raleigh.

Strategy:

Target single-family homes and properties suitable for tech professionals looking for quieter, suburban settings.

5. Fort Lupton, CO

Opportunity:

Denver's rapid growth and housing crunch could push more development into nearby cities like Fort Lupton.

Strategy:

Focus on land development and residential construction. There's potential for long-term appreciation as the area urbanizes.

6. Boulder City, NV

Opportunity:

Proximity to Las Vegas provides tourism-related opportunities, especially with increased interest in more residential properties and short-term rentals.

Strategy:

Consider vacation rentals, residential developments, and hospitality projects.

7. Tukwila, WA

Opportunity:

Seattle's tech-driven economy creates demand for housing and commercial spaces in surrounding areas like Tukwila.

Strategy:

Focus on multifamily housing and tech-related office space developments.

8. Decatur, GA

Opportunity:

As a close suburb of Atlanta, Decatur is poised for growth as Atlanta continues its expansion.

Strategy:

Invest in properties catering to young professionals and families. Mixed-use developments could also be a good fit.

9. Shawnee, OK

Opportunity:

The growing economy of Oklahoma City, driven by energy and healthcare, benefits Shawnee.

Strategy:

Focus on commercial real estate and residential developments that cater to middle-income families.

10. Pleasant Grove, UT

Opportunity:

Salt Lake City's booming tech industry could spill over into Pleasant Grove.

Strategy:

Target tech industry employees with affordable housing options, particularly single-family homes.

11. Newberg, OR

Opportunity:

Portland's urban sprawl and rising real estate prices create opportunities in nearby Newberg.

Strategy:
Invest in residential properties and consider mixed-use developments to cater to growing demand.

12. Apache Junction, AZ
Opportunity:
Proximity to Phoenix offers opportunities, especially for those looking for affordable housing outside of the city.
Strategy:
Given Arizona's popularity with retirees, focus on residential developments and potentially senior living communities.

13. Marlborough, MA
Opportunity:
Boston's high housing costs make Marlborough an attractive option for commuters.
Strategy:
Invest in rental properties and consider transit-oriented developments.

14. Beaumont, CA
Opportunity:
The Inland Empire's growth, driven by logistics and warehousing, benefits Beaumont.
Strategy:
Focus on residential developments and commercial properties catering to logistics workers.

15. Redmond, WA
Opportunity:
As a tech hub itself, Redmond is an attractive investment option near Seattle.

Strategy:
Invest in tech-related commercial real estate and upscale residential properties.

16. Dublin, CA

Opportunity:
Located near two major tech hubs, Dublin benefits from the overflow of professionals and businesses.

Strategy:
Focus on high-end residential and commercial properties catering to tech workers.

17. Herriman, UT

Opportunity:
Like Pleasant Grove, Herriman benefits from the tech boom in Salt Lake City.

Strategy:
Residential developments targeting tech workers and their families would be ideal.

18. Little Elm, TX

Opportunity:
The rapid expansion of Dallas is making Little Elm an attractive suburb.

Strategy:
Invest in family-friendly residential developments and commercial properties that cater to suburban lifestyles.

19. Apex, NC

Opportunity:
Like Holly Springs, Apex benefits from the growth of Raleigh's tech industry.

Strategy:
> Focus on single-family homes and rental properties targeting tech professionals.

20. Ankeny, IA

Opportunity:
> Des Moines' growth, driven by the finance and insurance sectors, is spilling over into Ankeny.

Strategy:
> Invest in multifamily residential properties and commercial spaces catering to professionals.

A Real-World Example

To illustrate the practical application of the satellite city investment strategy, let me share a recent investment I made. I recently acquired a triple-net lease property in Rock Hill, South Carolina, just 27 miles southeast of Charlotte, North Carolina.

Why Rock Hill?

Rock Hill perfectly embodies the satellite city principles:

Proximity to a Major Metro: At just 27 miles from Charlotte, Rock Hill is well within the 60-mile radius that characterizes an ideal satellite city investment.

Growth Potential: Rock Hill is strategically positioned to benefit from Charlotte's expansion. As Charlotte expands, the city will likely see an increase in population, job opportunities, and property values.

Affordability: Compared to Charlotte proper, Rock Hill offers more attractive property prices, allowing for potentially higher returns on investment.

Reduced Competition: While many investors focus on Charlotte, Rock Hill represents a less saturated market, offering better opportunities and less buyer competition.

The Charlotte-Rock Hill Connection

Charlotte is a major financial center and a rapidly growing metropolitan area.

As the city expands, I expect to see:

Population Spillover: As housing prices in Charlotte rise, more people may choose to live in Rock Hill and commute to Charlotte for work.

Business Expansion: Companies looking to expand or relocate from Charlotte may find Rock Hill attractive due to lower operating costs.

Infrastructure Development: As the region grows, improved transportation links between Charlotte and Rock Hill will likely further integrate the two cities.

Cultural and Economic Ties: Increased movement of people and businesses between the two cities will likely strengthen their economic and cultural connections.

The Investment Potential

My triple net lease property in Rock Hill represents a strategic implementation of the satellite city approach.

Stable Current Income: The triple net lease structure provides a steady, predictable income stream.

Long-term Appreciation: As Rock Hill benefits from Charlotte's growth, property values will likely appreciate over time.

Diversification: This investment allows me to tap into Charlotte's economic strength while diversifying away from the potentially overheated Charlotte real estate market.

Future Development Potential: As the area grows, there may be opportunities for property improvement or redevelopment to meet changing market needs.

The Importance of Established Tenants

A crucial aspect of this investment that I haven't mentioned yet is the tenant occupying the property. The triple net lease is with Chipotle, a well-known and established fast-casual restaurant chain.

Working with established tenants like Chipotle is a key strategy in triple net lease investments for several reasons:

Brand Recognition: Chipotle's strong brand recognition adds value to the property and can attract other businesses to the area.

Financial Stability: Established companies like Chipotle typically have solid financial foundations, reducing the risk of default on lease payments.

Long-Term Commitment: Well-established brands are more likely to sign longer lease terms, providing stable income over an extended period.

Property Maintenance: In a triple-net lease, the tenant is responsible for property maintenance. An established company like Chipotle has the resources and systems to maintain the property well.

Resale Value: Properties leased to recognized brands often have higher resale values due to the perceived stability and quality of the tenant.

By securing Chipotle as a tenant, this Rock Hill investment benefits from the satellite city approach and gains the added security and prestige of an established, nationally recognized brand.

With Chipotle as the tenant, this investment is a real-world example of how the satellite city approach can be combined with securing established tenants in triple-net lease arrangements to further reduce risk.

Rock Hill and similar cities are poised to reap the benefits as Charlotte grows and expands its influence.

This investment strategy allows us to stay ahead of the curve, capitalizing on growth trends before they fully materialize in property values and rental rates. The presence of a strong tenant like Chipotle adds an extra layer of security and potential for long-term appreciation.

INVESTMENT EDGE

Smaller cities near major metro centers offer a strategic opportunity to capture growth at its inception and leverage urban economic dynamics. By targeting the right properties and aligning with emerging trends, you can secure assets at attractive prices and gain substantial appreciation as the market matures.

Ultimately, this early-mover approach positions you to stay ahead of the curve without chasing overheated markets.

In investing, as in life, the greatest rewards
often come to those who dare to be different.

The Fast Lane to Exponential Wealth Growth

Few strategies can propel your net worth on a hockey stick trajectory, like acquiring an established business. With over 33 million small businesses in the U.S., the opportunities for wealth creation are vast and varied.

No matter the industry, one thing is sure: purchasing an existing business positions you for exponential growth and financial success.

It's a more direct route to building life-changing wealth than almost any other method.

Small Businesses Drive The Economy
99.9%
Of businesses in the U.S. are small businesses
Small Business. Big Employer.
45.9%
Of Americans are employed by small businesses
61.6M
Americans are employed by small businesses[66]

66   https://www.uschamber.com/small-business/small-business-data-center

Strategic Goal

This wealth-building approach focuses on acquiring businesses with a proven track record, enabling rapid financial growth by leveraging established success.

Instead of starting from scratch—which demands substantial time, effort, and risk—this strategy involves purchasing a profitable company with an established customer base and a foothold in the market.

By acquiring a successful business, you gain immediate access to cash flow, assets, and market presence, allowing you to generate income from day one.

This approach also allows you to take advantage of various financing options, like Small Business Administration (SBA) loans, enabling you to control a valuable asset with a relatively small investment. Using leverage—borrowed capital—you can amplify your returns and acquire a much larger business than you could otherwise afford.

The key is identifying businesses with solid fundamentals and growth potential, performing thorough due diligence, and managing the business effectively post-acquisition.

This strategy is a fast track to wealth and financial success that can significantly outpace traditional methods.

Let's break down the critical components.

Leverage Financing Options

One of the greatest advantages of acquiring an existing business is the ability to leverage financing options, which can amplify your returns.

For instance, with an SBA loan, you may need to put down only 10-20% of the purchase price, while the remaining 80-90%

is financed. For a business worth $1 million, this means an initial investment of $100,000 to $200,000. If the company is already profitable, cash flow should cover debt payments, making the acquisition self-sustaining.

The real power of leverage lies in using **other people's money (OPM)** to acquire assets. By financing most of the purchase, you can acquire a much larger and more established business than if you were starting from scratch with only your savings.

This not only accelerates your entry into the business world but also positions you to benefit from the existing cash flow, customer base, and business position with the market, all while potentially increasing your overall return on investment.

When used wisely, leverage maximizes investment potential, accelerating wealth creation beyond what's possible through organic growth alone.

Established Income Streams

When you acquire an existing business, you're not just buying assets or a brand—you're acquiring established income streams.

This is a significant advantage over starting a new business, which can often take years to become profitable.

With an existing business, revenue generation begins from day one, providing immediate cash flow that can be a game-changer for your financial strategy.

Not only will it allow you to take a salary, but you also receive two strategic benefits:

1. **You can reinvest in the business to fuel growth, building on an existing foundation of success.**

2. **You can use cash flow to cover debt payments, reducing financial strain and allowing the business to "pay for its purchase," reducing your financial burden.**

Reliable income streams reduce business ownership risks.

Cash flow can be reinvested to improve operations, expand, or develop new products and services, giving you a head start on further growth and innovation.

Unlike a startup, where the future is uncertain and the timeline to profitability is unclear, an existing business with a revenue track record provides a solid foundation to build.

This stability provides a strong foundation, allowing you to focus on scaling rather than surviving.

Acquiring a business with solid cash flow equips you to weather economic downturns or unexpected expenses. It's a key factor that can significantly contribute to the long-term success of your investment.

Established Brand Identity

Building a brand from the ground up requires time, resources, and patience. It involves everything from creating a recognizable logo and message to establishing a reputation and earning customers' trust—which I know can take years.

However, when you acquire an existing business, you inherit an established brand identity that typically includes loyal customers and a strong presence in the marketplace.

This lets you skip the costly, time-intensive brand-building process and focus on strategic growth.

A well-known brand identity also provides a competitive advantage, especially in industries or markets where brand loyalty is a key driver of consumer behavior.

This is valuable because brand equity directly contributes to steady revenue and resilience against market shifts. A strong brand differentiates the business, making it easier to retain customers and attract new ones.

A business with an established brand identity gives you a head start in the market.

Product-Market Fit

Acquiring a business provides you with a product-market fit from day one, bypassing the costly trial-and-error phase that many startups face. The business you're acquiring has already established a product or service that resonates with its target market, saving you the time and expense of finding a fit. This reduces the risk of failure and saves you from the costly and time-consuming process of validating the business model.

You can immediately shift your focus to **scaling the business, improving efficiencies, or expanding the product line**. Rather than worrying about whether the market will respond positively to your offerings, you can optimize and grow what's already working.

It's a significant head start, allowing you to focus on growth without the foundational risks of a startup.

Limited Downside Risk

Starting a business from scratch is fraught with risks, including the possibility of total failure due to unforeseen challenges and market miscalculations.

Acquiring an existing business significantly reduces this downside risk. You can review financial statements, customer contracts, and key performance metrics, which will give you a clear picture of the business's health.

When purchasing an existing business, you can negotiate the purchase price based on the company's historical performance and current market conditions. This allows you to enter the deal with a clearer understanding of the business's value and potential return on investment.

An established business with a proven track record allows you to secure favorable financing terms and further reduce financial risk, giving you a solid foundation to build upon.

Operator to Learn From

An often-overlooked benefit of acquiring an existing business is the chance to learn directly from the current owner or operator, who often stays on board during the transition. This provides invaluable insights into day-to-day operations, industry nuances, and intricacies of customer relationships.

This knowledge transfer reduces the learning curve, enabling you to enter your new role with a deeper understanding of the business's inner workings and how to capitalize on opportunities that may take time for an outsider to understand.

Learning from the operator gives you the confidence and expertise to run the business successfully.

This mentorship-like period is invaluable. It creates a smoother transition and can be instrumental in setting you up for long-term success.

Plans and Processes Already in Place

A key advantage of acquiring an established business is inheriting its existing plans, processes, and systems. **With well-established processes already in place, you avoid months—or even years—of foundational work**. Instead, you can focus on optimizing and expanding to drive growth.

This allows you to hit the ground running, directing attention to areas for improvement and increasing efficiency without the common pitfalls and steep learning curve of building a business from scratch.

Final Thoughts

Acquiring an existing business offers a running start on the path to wealth generation compared to starting from scratch.

By purchasing a profitable business, you skip many of the challenges and risks associated with startups and position yourself for immediate financial success.

Make your move — take the path that accelerates your wealth trajectory and puts exponential growth within reach.

There's A Reason It's Called Going Platinum

While this book highlights silver as the most obvious opportunity in the precious metals market, platinum is another metal I've been accumulating.

Platinum holds unique advantages as both a critical resource and a high-value strategic investment.

Recognizing its value and potential, I've steadily increased my exposure to platinum over the past few years, adding it to my long-term holdings.

In many ways, I consider platinum to be Silver 2.0.

	SILVER	PLATINUM
Investment Demand	✓	✓
Store of Value	✓	✓
Hedge against inflation	✓	✓
Safe haven against a weakening dollar	✓	✓
Essential for Modern Technology	✓	✓
Pivotal Role in Clean Energy Transition	✓	✓
Growing Demand	✓	✓
Supply Chain Vulnerability	✓	✓

Industrial Application

Driving the Future with Platinum

Platinum's role in the automotive industry is critical. Platinum is behind the scenes, powering technologies that reduce harmful emissions and improve vehicle efficiency.

Catalytic Converters: Platinum is the key ingredient that enables catalytic converters to clean vehicle exhausts, reduce harmful emissions, and help automakers meet stringent environmental regulations.

Spark Plugs: Platinum's high melting point and corrosion resistance make it perfect for the tips of high-performance spark plugs, ensuring longevity and reliability.

Platinum is the true workhorse in automotive innovation, driving the shift towards cleaner, more efficient vehicles.

The Catalyst for Progress

In the chemical industry, platinum is indispensable. It is a catalyst in many industrial processes, speeding up chemical reactions and improving efficiency. Platinum is pivotal in the production of:

Industrial and Household Chemicals: From nitric acid to nylon, platinum's catalytic properties are at the heart of manufacturing processes that create everyday products.

Silicone Production: Platinum compounds are essential for producing specialty silicones, which are used in everything from sealants and lubricants to electrical wire insulation.

Petroleum Refining: Platinum's catalytic capabilities also extend to refining crude oil, transforming low-grade fuels into high-efficiency gasoline, diesel, and jet fuel.

Platinum's unmatched effectiveness in these complex chemical processes makes it a cornerstone of industrial progress.

Platinum and Modern Technology

In electronics, platinum is crucial for enhancing performance and ensuring reliability. It's the unsung hero in:

Hard Disk Drives: Platinum coatings in hard drives allow for higher data storage densities, making your devices faster and more efficient.

Fiber Optic Cables: Platinum's presence in fiber optic cables supports the infrastructure that powers our digital world, enabling faster and more reliable internet connections.

As technology evolves, platinum's role will only become more vital, ensuring that our devices meet the ever-increasing demands of modern life.

Platinum's Lifesaving Applications

Platinum's biocompatibility and resistance to corrosion make it invaluable in the medical field.

It literally saves lives:

Medical Devices: From stents and catheters to pacemakers and defibrillators, platinum's durability ensures that these critical devices function reliably inside the human body.

Chemotherapy: Platinum compounds like cisplatin are used in chemotherapy drugs to treat various cancers, offering hope and life-saving treatment to countless patients.

Dental Fillings: Platinum's strength and biocompatibility make it an ideal material for durable dental fillings.

Platinum's significant contributions to healthcare make it not just a precious metal but a precious resource in medical innovation.

Other Industries: Platinum's Unrivaled Versatility

The uses of platinum extend far beyond the obvious, touching on industries where its unique properties are irreplaceable:

Glass Manufacturing: Platinum's high melting point and corrosion resistance make it essential for handling molten glass during the production of fiberglass and LCD glass.

Jewelry: With its silvery-white luster and resistance to tarnish, platinum is a favorite in the jewelry industry. It symbolizes luxury and durability.

Laboratory Equipment: Platinum is used in labs in high-temperature crucibles and thermocouples, providing reliability in extreme conditions.

Aerospace: Platinum coatings protect jet-engine blades from the extreme temperatures encountered during flight, ensuring the safety and efficiency of air travel.

Platinum at the Forefront of Clean Energy

As we move towards a more sustainable future, platinum's role in emerging technologies is becoming increasingly important:

Fuel Cells: Platinum is crucial in fuel cell technology, particularly in proton exchange membrane (PEM) fuel cells, which power the next generation of vehicles with clean energy.

Green Hydrogen Production: Platinum catalysts are vital in PEM electrolyzers, which produce green hydrogen from water using renewable energy sources—a critical step towards a sustainable hydrogen economy.

DID YOU KNOW:
Platinum is the only material suitable for the electrodes required in the 600,000 heart pacemakers that are implanted each year.[67]

---

67   https://platinuminvestment.com/about/platinum-facts

A Metal for the Future

Platinum's unique properties, critical industrial applications, and growing demand make it a compelling investment. Like silver, platinum is more than just a precious metal. It's a cornerstone of modern technology and a key player in the clean energy transition.

Like silver, platinum's unique properties make it irreplaceable in its applications. As a result, the platinum market is experiencing a shift similar to silver - limited supply and increasing demand.

As the world continues to embrace new technologies, particularly in clean energy, the demand for platinum is set to rise.

With all the similarities, what excited me the most about the investment potential of platinum is that:

1. **Platinum is both a critical mineral AND a critical material (Yes, two different things)**
2. **Platinum is scarce.**

Let's break these down so you understand why I believe platinum is silver on steroids.

Why Is Platinum Critical?

"The Energy Act of 2020 defines a "**critical material**" as:

> "Any non-fuel mineral, element, substance, or material that the Secretary of Energy determines: (i) has a high risk of supply chain disruption; and (ii) serves an essential function in one or more energy technologies, including technologies that produce, transmit, store, and conserve energy; or

A critical mineral, as defined by the Secretary of the Interior. The Energy Act of 2020 defines a "**critical mineral**" as:

Any mineral, element, substance, or material designated as critical by the Secretary of the Interior, acting through the director of the U.S. Geological Survey."[68]

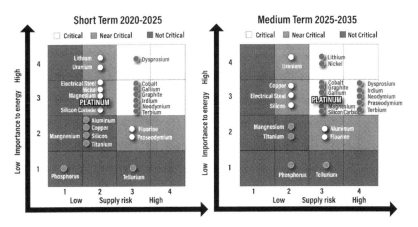

Platinum lands on both lists because it is essential for modern technology and national security. Should there be a disruption in the supply chain, its absence would have significant consequences.

When an application relies on Platinum, like silver, it can not be substituted for something else.

Platinum's classification as a critical material underscores its strategic importance.

When I see a material receive a critical designation from the government, as platinum has, I pay attention. This highlights the importance authorities place on securing reliable access to this resource.

---

68   https://www.energy.gov/cmm/what-are-critical-materials-and-critical-minerals

Knowing there's growing demand and potential supply disruptions, how many critical metals can you easily purchase?

Not many.

Even fewer with expanding uses.

Not only that, it's scarce!

Platinum is rarer than gold.

Platinum's rarity is one of the most significant factors contributing to its value proposition.

Unlike other precious metals, such as gold and silver, platinum is far less abundant in the earth's crust and has a lower annual production.

This inherent scarcity and its status as a key material in various industrial applications drive its value.

Geological Rarity

Platinum is approximately 30 times rarer than gold. It is found in only a few locations worldwide, with most platinum production concentrated in South Africa, accounting for nearly 70% of the global supply. Other significant sources include Russia and Zimbabwe, but the global output remains limited.

DID YOU KNOW: Platinum is one of the heaviest metals. A six-inch cube of platinum weighs as much as an average human being.[69]

---

69   https://platinuminvestment.com/about/platinum-facts

Why is Platinum so rare?

Platinum is rare because the specific geological conditions required for its formation make it much less common than other metals.

The challenges don't end with locating formations.

Platinum extraction presents significant challenges. It's not only scarce and difficult to locate, but mining also involves complex and costly operations. These often include deep underground excavations and substantial environmental hurdles to overcome.

Imagine one mine goes offline. What do you think is going to happen to the price?

Supply constraints + increased industrial demand = upward pressure on prices.

In the platinum, production costs help support the market price.

The annual production of platinum is significantly lower than that of gold and silver.

"Platinum may be as much as thirty times rarer than gold, with around 190 metric tons mined globally each year. Gold is far more abundant, with up to 3,300 metric tons mined annually around the world."[70]

One statistic that has always blown my mind: if you gathered up all the gold ever mined, it would fit in three Olympic-sized swimming pools.

Want to know how many swimming pools platinum would fill?

"If all the platinum ever mined were melted and poured into an Olympic-sized swimming pool, it would barely reach your ankles."[71]

---

70   https://www.unbiased.com/discover/investing/platinum-vs-gold-investment
71   https://science.howstuffworks.com/environmental/earth/geology/platinum.htm

That is an extreme rarity.

Am I diving into Platinum head first?

No.

Am I allocating some of my funds to it? You better believe it!

The market dynamics of platinum look good to me, and I want exposure to and a strategic position in this investment area.

As demand for platinum continues to grow across key industries and emerging technologies, I see significant upside potential.

Platinum's critical material status and its vulnerable supply chain, which is concentrated in a few countries, position it uniquely in the investment landscape. One supply shock could disrupt the entire market and spike prices.

And with recycling unable to meet the growing industrial demand for platinum, the market dynamics are driven by a delicate balance of powerful forces.

My opinion of this trade:

This is a strategic investment based on the premise that owning a critical resource facing potential supply challenges and increasing production hurdles will pay off significantly when the supply squeeze occurs.

And if you're wondering, the term "going platinum" is used metaphorically to indicate reaching a pinnacle of success, excellence, or value in various fields, much like how platinum itself is associated with rarity, prestige, and high worth.

Given its critical role and scarcity, platinum represents an unparalleled opportunity. Consider securing a position in platinum now before its value as a rare, essential metal escalates further.

PART 3
A New Era of Opportunity

Building a Lasting Foundation for Wealth

Building wealth requires a disciplined approach that aligns your investment strategy with both your financial goals and risk tolerance.

In the initial stages, focusing on foundational principles is essential to establishing a successful foundation.

Early success minimizes setbacks, making it easier to stay the course and work toward the future you envision.

The early stages are pivotal because setbacks and disruptions can quickly derail your progress.

It's essential to start strong, maintain focus, and avoid any disruptions that can derail progress.

Focus on four essential pillars:

1. Aligning Investments with Goals
2. Executing with precision
3. Adapting to Market Changes
4. Preparing for Any Scenario

These pillars lay the groundwork for everything you'll build upon as you move forward.

In the following sections, we'll examine these areas in detail to help you achieve your financial aspirations.

Tailoring Investments to Your Goals

Aligning your investment choices with your financial goals and risk tolerance is essential to building resilience. Each decision should be a purposeful step toward your bigger objectives—whether it's early retirement, substantial wealth accumulation, or creating a lasting legacy.

Personalizing Your Investment Portfolio

- **Risk Assessment:** Gauge your comfort with various risk levels. Knowing your tolerance helps you stay confident during market ups and downs.
- **Goal Alignment:** Set measurable financial goals and tailor your strategy to support them. Aligning your investments with your life goals ensures your portfolio works for you, not against you. Set both short- and long-term financial goals, with measurable milestones to track your progress. This provides direction and keeps your investment choices targeted.
- **Asset Allocation:** Choose the right mix of asset classes to balance risk and return. Diversifying your investments across various categories ensures no single asset dominates, supporting stability and growth.

Strategic Planning and Execution

Wealth-building goes beyond selecting the right investments—it's about executing your strategy with precision. Success demands a clear plan, disciplined action, and well-timed decisions.

Strategic planning and execution turn ideas into successful outcomes.

The key to wealth-building lies not only in your choices but in how you execute them.

Planning and Execution Tactics:

- **Develop a Clear Investment Thesis:** For each asset, articulate why it deserves a place in your portfolio. Is it undervalued? Does it offer robust growth potential? Or does it serve as a hedge against market volatility? Knowing *why* you're investing and *how* each asset fits into your broader financial objectives keeps your decisions focused and strategic.
- **Master Entry and Exit Strategies:** Timing can make or break your investment success. Establish clear criteria for both when to buy and when to sell. This isn't about chasing the market but making calculated moves that align with your strategy. Set specific entry conditions based on valuation, market trends, or technical indicators to ensure you enter at favorable moments. Similarly, a strong exit plan is essential. This could mean selling at a target price, using stop-loss orders, or establishing a time-based milestone. A clear exit strategy prevents you from holding onto assets too long or selling too soon due to market fear.
- **Execute with Discipline:** Discipline is the backbone of successful investing. Stick to your plan, even when market volatility or unexpected events stir emotions. Resist the urge to make impulsive decisions based on short-term fluctuations. Instead, rely on the criteria you've established to guide your actions. By executing your strategy with discipline and precision, you optimize

your wealth-building efforts, manage risks effectively, and stay on course to achieve your financial goals. Market fluctuations are inevitable. Building mental resilience and focusing on long-term outcomes help prevent emotionally driven decisions.

Adapting to Market Shifts

Flexibility and adaptability are essential in the ever-changing world of investing, where markets are influenced by numerous factors, from economic indicators to technological shifts.

Successful navigation—especially when employing a contrarian strategy—requires the ability to adjust one's approach as conditions evolve.

Flexibility is the hallmark of successful investors.

Those who can swiftly adjust their strategies in response to market dynamics thrive in volatile environments.

In investing, as in life, the ability to adapt is often the difference between success and failure.

Strategies for Adapting to Market Changes:

- **Leveraging Technology:** Utilize advanced tools like AI and machine learning to analyze market data and trends. These technologies can provide faster and more accurate insights, giving you an edge in decision-making.
- **Diversification Tactics:** Stay ready to adjust your asset mix in response to market conditions. This might involve rotating between sectors, increasing exposure to specific geographies, or shifting focus to alternative assets.
- **Maintaining Alignment:** Regular rebalancing keeps your portfolio aligned with your goals. Rebalancing allows you to lock in gains by selling off some overperforming

assets and reallocating the proceeds to underweighted areas, maintaining your desired risk-return balance.

- **Capitalizing on Opportunities:** Market shifts often create opportunities to buy undervalued assets. You can take advantage of these opportunities, potentially increasing your returns.
- **Anticipate Economic Downturns:** Downturns are an inevitable part of the market cycle, and how you prepare for them can significantly impact your ability to protect and grow your investments. Preparing for economic shifts involves a combination of strategic diversification, liquidity management, and hedging strategies to ensure your portfolio remains resilient in the face of uncertainty.

Maintaining a 'Rogue' Mindset

Always prepared. Always ready.

A 'rogue' mindset isn't just advantageous—it's essential for outmaneuvering the market. Embrace constant vigilance, adaptability, and the willingness to take a different path when needed.

Here's how to cultivate these attributes and stay prepared for everything.

Preparedness Tactics:

- **Continuous Vigilance and Regular Reviews:** Markets are dynamic and constantly influenced by various factors. To stay ahead, maintain a sharp awareness of what's happening within your portfolio and the broader economic landscape. Conduct frequent assessments of your investment strategies and portfolio performance.

Regular assessments help you pivot when necessary, seizing opportunities or mitigating risks in real-time.

- **Building a Strong Network:** A strong network of like-minded individuals and industry experts is invaluable. It provides fresh perspectives, early insights into emerging trends, and crucial support during challenging times. Connect with other investors who share your contrarian (non-mainstream) mindset. These relationships foster the exchange of ideas and collaboration on investment opportunities, deepening your understanding of market dynamics. Build relationships with advisors and experts—their insight will help you stay informed about the latest developments and navigate complex decisions.

- **Cultivating Emotional Resilience:** Market volatility is inevitable, and emotional resilience is critical to staying during turbulent times. The ability to remain calm and stick to your plan can make the difference between success and failure. When markets are volatile, it's easy to make impulsive decisions based on fear or greed. Emotional resilience means staying grounded and avoiding knee-jerk reactions that could derail your long-term goals. In times of volatility, stay focused on long-term objectives. This perspective will help you manage short-term fluctuations without losing sight of your end goals.

- **Prepare for Any Scenario:** Prepare for any scenario, whether it's an economic downturn, sudden market correction, or personal emergency. Maintain a pool of liquid assets or an emergency fund that you can access quickly without disrupting your investment strategies. This financial cushion protects you in case of unexpected expenses or market disruptions. Stay informed about the legal and tax implications of your investments. Plan for the future by establishing clear wealth transfer strategies. This might involve estate planning, establishing trusts, or other methods to preserve your legacy. Implement proactive wealth transfer strategies like trusts or estate planning to protect and align your legacy with your values.

Final Thoughts

Building wealth is a continuous journey that requires adaptability and discipline.

With countless opportunities ahead, you're prepared to seize control of your financial future.

Stay resilient and disciplined, and approach each decision with clarity—these are the cornerstones of a wealth-building journey that endures.

Conclusion

Formula for success: rise early, work hard, strike oil.
~J. Paul Getty

The Beginning of Your Journey

Congratulations! You've reached the end of this book—and the beginning of an exciting new chapter.

Throughout these pages, we've uncovered the extraordinary potential of silver—a resource poised to reshape our world as profoundly as oil transformed the 20th century. But what you've gained goes far beyond understanding a precious metal. You now hold a blueprint for building lasting wealth in an ever-changing world—a future of abundance and freedom you will actively create, not passively inherit.

Consider the skills you now possess:

- The ability to spot emerging trends before they become apparent to the masses.
- A framework for managing risk that protects and grows your wealth.

- The critical thinking skills to evaluate opportunities others miss.
- Most importantly, the mindset of a wealth creator rather than a passive observer.

This knowledge isn't just about investing in silver—it's about investing in yourself. Move forward with confidence, knowing you are the architect of your future and can shape opportunities rather than chase them.

The world is transforming at an unprecedented pace, creating new paths to prosperity daily. But here's the crucial truth: wealth flows to those who act. The future belongs not to the hesitant but to the bold—those who recognize opportunity and seize it with both hands.

You stand at a crossroads. Behind you lies the familiar path of conventional thinking. Ahead stretches a new path full of opportunities leading to financial independence and true freedom. You now have the map, the tools, and the knowledge to navigate this journey successfully.

The choice is yours, and the time is now.

Remember, wealth rewards those who take bold steps.

Begin today, and claim the opportunities within reach.

Your VIP Access Awaits!

Scan the code to unlock special insider content and be the first to know about precious metals news and exclusive offers.

Join our community of savvy investors who always stay a step ahead.